John Riley

Selected Poetry & Prose

Selected Poetry & Prose

'*The absolute is a room*'

JOHN RILEY

edited by Ian Brinton

Shearsman Books

This edition first published in the United Kingdom in 2016 by
Shearsman Books
50 Westons Hill Drive
Emersons Green
BRISTOL
BS16 7DF

Shearsman Books Ltd Registered Office
30–31 St. James Place, Mangotsfield, Bristol BS16 9JB
(this address not for correspondence)

ISBN 978-1-84861-488-8

Works by John Riley reproduced here are
copyright © the Syndics of Cambridge University Library, 2016.

Introduction copyright © Ian Brinton, 2016.
Preface copyright © Ian Duhig, 2016.

The right of John Riley to be identified as the author of this work has been asserted by his Estate in accordance with the Copyrights, Designs and Patents Act of 1988.
All rights reserved.

ACKNOWLEDGEMENTS

The provenance of all previously published works reprinted here may be found in the Notes on pp.122-123. Previously unpublished works have been sourced from the Cambridge University Library MS Add. 10038 and are included here by permission of the Syndics of Cambridge University Library.

*To Kay, as ever,
and to
Kostas Madalaras*

Contents

Ian Duhig: Preface	7
Ian Brinton: Introduction	10

Ancient and Modern

Ancient and Modern	19
Views of Where One Is	19
Pentecost	20
After the Music	20
This Time of Year	21

What Reason Was

For Gordon and Hélène Jackson	25
The Full Moon is Bathing These Fields	25
A Picture : an Historical Perspective	26
Song	26
Dream Poem	27
A Birthday Poem for One Person, and Hence for Others	27
What Reason Was for the Animal	28
Bright Feast, the Desert in a Pagan Year	29
The Shortest Day, Riding Northward	29
The Attraction	30
The World Itself, the Long Poem Foundered	31
Untitled	32
Spring Poem	32
Fragment	33
From the Russian of Osip Mandelstam	33
A Poem of Beginnings	34
The Poem as Light	34
Days at the Museum	35
Of the Baroque	36
An Anniversary	37
Poem on These Poems	38

Ways of Approaching

in memoriam	43
Prelude	43
Serious Exercise, in Honour of Boris Pasternak	47
open house	48
Report, Unfinished	48
Poem	52
Poem in Four Parts	52
poem for Jane	54
in memoriam Charles Olson	54
Rough Tor, Cornwall, this landscape what song	55
[untitled]	56
lines from a notebook : a reading	56

Czargrad   61

That is today

[Untitled]	73
at the Stanley Spencer exhibition	74
movement in three parts	74
travel notes	75
spring . diversion	76
summer seeming	77
for home again	79

Translations

Osip Mandelstam: Three Early Poems	83
Mandelstam's Octets	84
Mandelstam: The Stalin Ode Sequence	87
Boris Pasternak: Insomnia	98

Prose Pieces

Living In	101
How To	109
The Pig and Whistle Section	110
Down by the River Side	114

Notes   122
A List of John Riley's Works   124

Preface

'Riley's Light', the Leeds University celebration of the poet's work organised in 2015 by Helen Mort, to whom we remain immensely grateful, was represented by contributors ranging in age from Andrew McMillan and Vahni Capildeo to Peter Riley. Matthew Sperling, another contributor, also noted the range of publishers represented at the event including Cape, Carcanet, Chatto, Gallery from Ireland, Peepal Tree Press of the Caribbean and its diaspora, and Picador. Now Shearsman is represented and John Riley himself returns to print with this marvellous selection by Ian Brinton. Also in the audience at Leeds were poets as different as Michael Haslam and Paul Farley while Luke Kennard and Michael Symmons Roberts expressed considerable support although they were unable to attend. As well as the broad range of interest shown on that day, what made me confident that Riley's work would finally return to print was meeting Ian Brinton in person, whom I knew from his articles on Riley for various magazines over the years; I discovered that at a more immediate level, Ian had rescued the John Riley archive (now in Cambridge) from his widow Carol's nursing home, where it ran the risk of being dumped in the event of her death, at a time when she was in very fragile health. 'Riley's Light' took place in an atmosphere of celebration of the poet's achievements but it was also tinged with great sadness, as Carol Riley Brown had died the preceding week; happy to see a new stirring of broad-based enthusiasm for her husband's work, we can only imagine the pleasure this publication would have brought her.

Sometime earlier, Carol had personally chosen her husband's widely-admired 'Poem for Rilke in Switzerland' to be set by Mike McInerney, which was re-recorded and made available again after 'Riley's Light' by Choros Gregorianos in their memory, an act of recovery foreshadowing that of this book. 'Poem' was also one the first of Riley's that dazzled me as it does many others when I show it to them, with its extraordinary conclusion:

> The shock of re-
>
> Turning to myself after a long journey,
> With music, has made me cry, cry out — angels
> And history through the heart's attention grow transparent.

I mention all this here in tribute to a unique love suffusing this book, a poetry coming to prominence now against a background of cruel losses.

Leeds was John Riley's birthplace to which he returned after important years in Cambridge and subsequent teaching, but it is also where his talent was violently extinguished in 1978 at the age of only forty one. I can't even guess at what we have lost because of this; as Ian Brinton's selection here demonstrates, Riley was at this point engaged in those poetry-in-prose alchemical experiments we have only recently become familiar with in this country. I contacted Tim Longville over 'Riley's Light', who like Michael Haslam stressed that the results moved beyond prose poetry into something new, and Tim was also keen for John Riley to be remembered as a Leeds poet alongside the international reach of his achievement. There is a strange poetry within the stark prose of his hometown, where I now live and discovered John Riley's astonishing poems. David Wheatley made the interesting suggestion in his paper for 'Riley's Light' that perhaps Leeds shared something of the eternal city reflected in 'Czargrad': "With his studied non-specificity, Riley does bring something democratic and ubiquitous to his 'City of God'." Riley joined the Russian Orthodox Church here only for convenience sake, to practice, and was buried by Polish Orthodox rites, an important distinction bearing in mind the performance of those two institutions in the Second World War. A memoir is being prepared describing Riley's complex religious views, but here I merely wish to observe how it is an almost apophatic theological paradox in itself that our poet most of light has suffered so much darkness, from his own violent death to the destruction of most stocks of his books in the IRA bombing of Manchester. Nevertheless, his poetry of crystalline intellectual poise, shivering with its own harmonics of hesitations, survived the blows and the bombs, the eclipse and silence following his death. This is largely due to efforts by Riley's friends and admirers whom I don't have room to thank individually here, but his reputation had also established itself abroad, particularly in the U.S.A., whose poets were crucial to Riley's own development. Irish poets figure in this story too and Peter Sirr has written well of Riley's distinctive pitch between personal and divine love at a time when few of his contemporaries explored spiritual and emotional complexities, let alone in Riley's visionary and highly-original way.

In fact, there has been no poet like John Riley since his time either, although if you are new to his work, you will notice traces of his influence on many poets after you read this book, particular in the younger generation. Its publication makes available to a larger audience the work of a poet brilliant in so many ways, enhancing our understanding of poetry after the Second World War but also enriching our poetry's present and future if we will in turn give it the heart's attention it deserves.

Ian Duhig

Introduction

Judgement, like an epiphany, comes unexpectedly and, according to 'spring . diversion', one of John Riley's last published poems, 'so does glory / ready or not'. The chanting from a children's game of hide and seek suggests that we are not only the pursuers after truth and beauty but also the pursued and in the same poem we are presented with a spiritual conundrum that is central to Riley's poetry:

> the absolute is a room
> without doors or windows

The opening lines of his major poem, 'Czargrad', raise a question of Heideggerian proportions as knowledge of *dasein* is incorporated within a sentence which is already *on the move*

> to get to know the flight of birds, blossoming
> of lilac-bush tipped with white flame
> see the movement of the wind and try
> to reassemble quietness from the creakings of the house at night…

There is a sense of the spiritual here, as in so much of Riley's work, and a tracing of the unchanging eternal perceived through the transient noises of the now. Andrew Crozier, in his contribution to Tim Longville's collection of writings *For John Riley*, pointed to a 'dogmatic or magisterial' quality to much of this poetry 'in which the commonplaces of human experience become realistic emblems of man's spiritual nature'. Within this context it should come as no surprise that Riley's name should have become associated with that of the thirteenth-century Bishop of Lincoln, Robert Grosseteste, whose own short treatise *De Luce* ('On Light') merged an Aristotelian terminology with a concern for matter as substance. The light of which Grosseteste wrote was not the ordinary physical light of everyday experience but was a simple substance, almost spiritual in its properties. There was a distinction in the philosopher's work between *lux* and *lumen*, the former being light in its source, whereas the latter referred to reflected or radiated light. In John Riley's terms *lumen* was inseparable from *lux* and it still strikes one as appropriate that Michael Grant, a friend of Riley's from Cambridge days, should have opened his Afterword to the 1995 Carcanet Press edition of the *Selected Poems* with a reference to this preoccupation.

Grant pointed out that the 1970 poem, 'The Poem As Light', 'does not merely describe light: the poem's language appears informed by it, seeming to participate in the world that it invokes and delineates'. It was in the first section of that poem that Riley introduced the reader to a 'dream / Of Byzantium', that city which in turn became Czargrad, and referred to Art as 'the building, moved in, breathed in'.

Grant's introductory comments also drew attention to the importance of icons for John Riley and writing about Russian Orthodoxy, the Church to which John Riley sought admission, Nicholas Zernov suggested that icons were not merely paintings within the Russian Orthodoxy:

> They were dynamic manifestations of man's spiritual power to redeem creation through beauty and art The colours and lines of the icons were not meant to imitate nature; the artists aimed at demonstrating that men, animals, and plants, and the whole cosmos, could be rescued from their present state of degradation and restored to their proper 'Image'... The artistic perfection of an icon was not only a reflection of the celestial glory — it was a concrete example of matter restored to its original harmony and beauty, and serving as a vehicle of the spirit. The icons were part of the transfigured cosmos.

This was perhaps part of what Riley's friend, Mike Chamberlain, was suggesting when he wrote to him in November 1971 about the 'endless quest to make piety formal, leaving words open for the reader but helping him to avoid making ironic selections.' Referring to an icon in the closing lines of 'Czargrad II' the poet presents the reader with a 'bright cloud' that is 'fixed'

>   that love
>   is never fulfilled
>   but the ways
>   of approaching
>   endless

The connection between stillness and movement, the phenomenology of the world as set against the light emanating from the icon, was caught for Riley in that section of the poem where he referred to 'keeping house, a few precious objects / clarities, the form of gratitude'. The 'gathered circle of light' which immediately followed this line is also a reminder of an iconic presentation.

Ezra Pound's awareness of the significance of light was central to his essay on Guido Cavalcanti:

> We appear to have lost the radiant world where one thought cuts through another with clean edge, a world of moving energies *'mezzo oscuro rade'*, *'risplende in sè perpetuale effecto'*, magnetisms that form, that are seen, that border the visible, the matter of Dante's *paradiso*, the glass under water, the form that seems a form seen in a mirror, these realities perceptible to the sense, interacting…

As John Riley would have been aware, one of the striking images in the opening Canto of Dante's *Paradiso* was the contrast between 'terra quïete' and 'foco vivo', earthly stillness within living flame. The connection between the stillness of Art and the Life Force which prompts it, diffusion of Light, is there too in Canto IX where we 'contemplate the art that makes beautiful the great result, and discern the good for which the world above wheels about the world below'.

Grant had referred to Pound's ambition 'to write in such a way that language might once again manifest this radiant energy, this fructifying and vivifying light, of which Erigena and Grosseteste had spoken'. He went on to suggest that Pound's 'practice leads us to believe that the energy for which he sought manifests itself only in stillness, and to a scrupulously vigilant and concentrated attention'. Part IV of 'Czargrad' was to conclude with the 'slight stir of air through grasses' bringing back to our minds the 'delicate' wind 'through silken corn' from the poem's second section.

In *Ways of Approaching*, and appearing between 'Poem In Four Parts' and 'Czargrad', Riley placed his 'in memoriam Charles Olson' with its reference to love as 'the mover or the move'

>   the stain of it
> in the midst of struggle , the story in the
> mouth with figures

The world of Art / Poetry is like the impression left on paper, the 'stain', the 'move' prompted by the 'mover', the Byzantine *troparion* or *kantakion*, hymns shining out from the icon and this highlights one important connection between Riley and Olson: a belief in the *polis*. The first two sections of 'Czargrad' had appeared in *Grosseteste Review* where they had attracted the attention of J.H. Prynne who was prompted to write to Tim Longville about the poem and some of the letter was then used as a flyer for the publication of the later four-part sequence. Prynne had referred to the possibility of some readers of 'Czargrad' dismissing the poem as 'maudlin theism…cathected into the lyric stream' but concluded that the 'dangers of this are part of the risk we are part of'. With a reference to the early Greek mystic Hierotheos Prynne suggested that Riley's 'Czargrad' was 'speechless above speech', echoing the early Christian's transportation wholly outside himself through his deep absorption with the sacred things celebrated in hymnology. In February 1963, after reading Olson's *Mayan Letters*, Prynne had written to Olson:

> I have a profound suspicion of this golden severance of sequence, that the past is idealised by standing beyond the reach of knowledge (not the reach of science & museum teams, but the passage of the imagination). To travel to the geographic of it is in part enactive of retrogression; but how to "come in quite fresh from the other end", to the choking beauty of inaccessibly remote nouns…The mass and weight of it, this is no less than the truth; but (from outside and afar) does this exclude the gerund of it: the stone, and also not far off, the sea?

The centrality of Grosseteste's work for the author of 'Czargrad' is perceived in the noise made by the 'wind' in the second section of the poem:

delicate the wind through silken corn

The movement of this diffusion, 'hills over hills', a sound ('the sighing of the wind') becomes matter 'weighty in the palm'. This wind is perceived as 'wisdom' which 'hovers' and cannot be held despite its tangibility 'between sense and idea / the cupped hands'; the gesture of receiving in 'cupped hands' allows us a sense of knowledge ('to get to know'). The elegiac sense of loss is hinted at with the juxtaposition of the 'wonders of the brain' that can hear music and multiple softness with the recognition that the 'music' has 'gone'

> gone, gone, but here and the form

If there is still an echo from that polis of spiritual awareness it rests now within the form of poetry, the 'music of the line'. However, this realisation in Riley is followed immediately with a reservation, an awareness that art itself may provide a trick like 'man's art we heard / a priest chant vespers to an empty church (save / for us, spectators) God / in the City.' The poetic echo here is from the concluding section of Eliot's *The Wasteland* with its chapel which is empty and yet the wind's home. As the cock stands on that chapel's roof, reminding us of St. Peter's denial of Christ, his calls prompt the arrival of rain.

Writing to Grant at the end of December 1976 Riley made some comments about the world of modern poetry which brought into focus his state of mind at that point, after the completion of 'Czargrad':

> It's difficult to know quite where to begin, but for me a sense of extreme dissatisfaction with the kind of poetry that is being written now, here, gives onto it. So much of it, not only the Larkins and Brownjohns, comes out of the 'individual' — what is uniquely 'mine' and what 'I' — or more usually — 'I personally' have to say… the man who is governed by his nature and acts in the strength of his natural qualities, of his 'character', is the least personal. He sets himself up as an individual, proprietor of his own nature, which he pits against the natures of others and regards as his 'me', thereby confusing person and nature… The poem is always grounded in the 'authenticity' of the self — usually by a language guaranteed to convince us of that authenticity — its honesty, sincerity etc.… citing of details, or the fact that 'I' am writing this poem… The effect of this is to make a fetish out of the created world and to blind us to what is truly Other. It seems to me the proper business of the poem… does not affirm the 'reality' of the world, it <u>negates</u> it. The poem is a turning which <u>literally</u> turns the reader with it — literally con-verts him; the reader is called into the poem so that together, reader and text, a movement of the spirit takes place.

Acknowledgements

I am grateful to the Syndics of Cambridge University Library for permission to publish copyright material that was donated to the Library by Carol Riley Brown.

Selected Poetry & Prose of John Riley

'The absolute is a room'

Ancient and Modern

For Pamela

Ancient and Modern

Away from the house the snow falls slanting,
And trees almost in leaf in yesterday's sun
Put on today an elegant new shape,
A complex, streamlined growth. Did you ever see

The maidenhair (some few survive), a pre-
Historic tree? Limpid leaf, irregularity,
A touching intent to grow come what may
With perhaps insufficient means: a pleasure

To look on. As who shall see in winter leisure
Compassionate history take lucid measure
Of our too-obvious nourishment on hate,
And love that can't pass for understanding.

Views of Where One Is

Go by train from here in any direction
And the land is flat: but imagination
Like Mount Tabor is above us all to see

As if on the horizon, so distantly

Trees like maps of intricate green continents
Floating in blue oceans: a constant movement
From mechanical habit to consciousness

Distantly, distantly, on the horizon.

Pentecost

In the night the struggle of men is not heard
And here I am at almost thirty walking in it.

The animals we have not yet managed to banish
Cry and are doubtless lonelier for our lights.

Were they gathered in one room or under sky
When the cloven tongues as of fire descended?

They were all with one accord come in one place.
At any rate they heard the sound as of a

Rushing mighty wind. How far we've walked since then.
I hear a nightjar's crying by the roadside

It cries and my passing doesn't disturb it
So near it makes the moonlit night less lonely.

After the Music

After the evening's music comes a storm.
    The lower air so fills with light and thunder
    I wonder the air itself does not catch light.

It's filled by vertical rain and insects crawl
For shelter under night-green leaves: passions fall.

Meanwhile Americans and Russians walk in
Slow motion one hundred and eighty miles up.

A space a world to move in as in music.
    A given time and strict measure to resolve this
    Curious involvement, a dominant species.

This Time of Year

Autumn can keep very very quiet
The mid-day sun hotter
Than ever summer was
Hot mist curls into trees

Form is deceptive
At last the days bite
My room is heated all day
Evenings turn into night

All love stops but mine
Goes on I said
And I was wrong
And I was right

The days bite deeper
Poets are such liars
What do they know of love
More than its absences

I stop to admire
The sky through an arch of branches
And thinking to go higher
Am caught in this gesture of pleasure

Appreciate the sagging hayrick
Its antiquated cottage form
Destined to keep cattle warm
Through winter

How much deeper must the days bite yet
There is a region where it doesn't matter
In the receding sky
Our gestures point to it.

What Reason Was

poems 1967-1969

So far love is for man what reason was for the animal world: it exists in its rudiments or tokens, but not as yet in fact
  — Vladimir Sergeyevich Solovyov

For Gordon and Hélène Jackson

In this room, to which the voices of the children of the house
Still penetrate, the father has painted the emaciated face

Of a hermit monk, traced with great interest his tangled white
Hair and beard, his apathetic eyes and sunken cheeks.

By now we demonstrate in guises other than the real
What's vital, an iron in the blood, some holiness

Completely unexpected. The children's crying. This snow at Easter.

> At their age at our age at any age shield us
> From the savagery of judging others.

The Full Moon Is Bathing These Fields

The full moon is bathing these fields richly.
I did not think that I would pass this way again.

Earlier, cloud spirals centred on the setting sun –
Say, shall we see this sky as an astronaut would see it
If one landed on our planet, its floes its continents and depths
So touchingly reduced to dimensions, charted?

Rats too closely herded kill each other or themselves,
Even those families enjoying the Roman peace of rats.
Pity the astronaut, that social man happy
Perhaps, to live our lowest fantasy.

If one landed on our earth. The noise of the wind in a tree
Startled me, it sounded exactly like a conversation.
But then none of nature is hostile.
Walk where you fear to walk, while you can.

A Picture : an Historical Perspective

Samuel van Hoogstraten's "View down a Corridor".

Only the bannisters in the foreground and the cat
At first seem at all domestic. Perspectives
Of a high-polished floor, black and white squares
Throwing back the light, no trace even of the cat's pawmarks.

To the side, in one of the many alcoves, seen it may be
In a mirror, a back view of a seated man
Formally upright, in high hat. And then,
And this one sees not in a mirror, beside him

The head and shoulders of a woman,
No expression at all on her very comely face.
And one realises who they are, the house
Is a home, and expression unnecessary.

The picture is now in Gloucestershire.

Song

Wasps and bees crack against the windowpanes.
Insects never learn about glass.

No more can I see through your absence.

Any stone flung in a river
Shatters the moon's reflection.

May we be reunited.

Dream Poem

I came to find you you were living
in a street with fences round the gardens.
I asked after you they told me
untrue things, it made me angry.

Then I found you it was like
meeting myself and I said let's
plant roses and carnations and you said
how shall we set about moving these fences?

A Birthday Poem for One Person, and Hence for Others

    1

The rainbow colours of becoming,
A rhythm of moving limbs and exchanged glances –

It is a part of it that the time for that is past,
I speak now of a still life.

A heron takes off as if pulled by strings let down from heaven;
A crow, pulled down more solidly by earth, repeatedly uses his wings.

But it is not that. Allegory is merely pretty.
Does movement suppose a resting place and if

It does can it be borne? It is gone, what was,
The touch the smell the sight are gone and the question

Where are they now is not the same as the question
Will she ever come back to me though the pressure

In both cases is equal and both play their part
In forcing me to this, and in the reticence involved.

2

So much that happened, my dear, is quite unthinkable
And how should I live through it without you.

Those who survive survive because they survive. Merely.
And that is not it, either: we have done more than that.

And more often now it is difficult to live, knowing that.
And how should I address you, when what we have is not to be held by this?

I think it is impatience drives me on as earth pulls down,
I think it is your absence gives a sweet stillness to it,

And it is memory saying all things must be changed.

3

Yes, but to get beyond this point?

I do not speak of accident, forgetfulness, for weakness
Of this kind is always with us and complaint supposes

No alteration. The point we have reached
Is not an argument, it is a greeting,

As gentle and as loving as I can make it
To you, today, beyond all changing days.

What Reason Was for the Animal

Enchanted merely by the morning dew
En route, night is past whenever we think it.

Grass trees bushes spread themselves in heaven.
A fox when free is captive of the kingdom.

I think we should pray for suicides more often.
I think we should pray for ourselves more often –

Wings not condemned or preordained
To flap around where there's nothing for them.

And this one morning the measure of all things.

Bright Feast, the Desert in a Pagan Year

It is that day of spring when all nature dies,
Bright Feast, the desert in a pagan year.

By no effort can we bear the unbearable,
By no lies make love convenient.

Yesterday I buried you whom tomorrow I shall raise up.
I shall resurrect you whom yesterday I crucified.

By no effort can we bear the unbearable,
By no lies make love convenient.

This therefore is the poem I make for you,
Today this is the poem I've made for you.

It is that day of spring when all of nature dies,
The Feast of Feasts, the desert in a pagan year.

The Shortest Day, Riding Northward

Being driven from where I want to be.
Earth swings east. Layer
After layer of air is lit.
Reluctantly. Not for long.

Let us drop pretence of images.
Let us live barely.
In more than a pagan triumph.
I have not loved you enough.

The Attraction

The attraction of well-washed hands and young words.
Hands eyes emotions in confined spaces.
The hill seems clean, the houses on top of it we ignore.

Smoke in the valley too proclaims a settlement.
Even the glances of the very poor at the moderately rich
Are timid. Always with us. Settled in.

Those men conferring on the river bank –
Are they going to shoot something? They are
Planning to build a city. Some trees are spared.

A bird's nest holds itself in a winter tree.
Forgive us our clothes our houses our bridges, they are misleading.
I go to my love. She lives by a stream.

Forgive us our morals forgive us our practices, they are inhuman.
The end of love as the end of a journey
Is that two things should be one.

Beauty enough *en route* is what no man can be sure of
And yet in mimic motion he can be surer of no thing else.
There is still some snow about. My love lives by a stream.

The World Itself, the Long Poem Foundered

The beating of my heart ripples the lamp.
Oh this constant expectation of good news.

A daisy grows. A girl passes. A girl passes along
The wet night street, the houses opposite are luminous.

The sky appears colourless but it is not so,
It could be a love, or longing, or both of these.

*

In full voice, in full throat, in full cry, in full
Flight. To trace, round-eyed, the flight of birds,

As a poet said. How to trace longing beyond sight,
Removed beyond sensible reaching? And to give it voice?

Perhaps, high up, the clouds are frozen rain,
And the stars – we read time backwards, watching it go by.

*

You would not believe how the birds sing round our home.
How easy to consider beauty timeless.

I know of no longing to appease this longing, be it even
Your voice, moving me to a celebration of it, love.

*

A stillness encompassing movement.
With enormous beauty still to answer to.

Blackness seeps through the closed door, douses the lamp.
It is a longing for the same world, and a different world.

Untitled

Let us love while the sunlight lasts.
By night the moon will light us.
Where is the moon's disc, in you?

Clouds move between the moon and me,
I watch them, not stirring from my chair.
Your hair, your brow, your eyes.

Your eyes, your face. Our slow time.
A driving wind sweeps the market-place bare.
It is intolerable, that you should die.

Rain, rain, rain, rain.

Spring Poem

Each individual flower, the yellow, the purple, the white,
And green spikes where later the red tulips will come.
Further along, the daffodils. The wind opposes them,
As it opposes me. It is our condition.

Each year I come to see them: now they've chopped down
Some of those trees at the end, it is not quite the same.
And if it were – did anything happen to me here
More memorable than taking pleasure in the spring?

Who sings of spring, sings of the March wind that opposes him.
Each individual flower, the yellow, the purple, the white,
And that delicate blue flower, would serve as a bouquet for her.

*

The trees are greening, the fallen sun stronger.
Pigeons cooing on the roof, love passes, passes through.

The world splits green to meet you.
My lady of gentleness, saving beauty.

*

Sweet violet, *viola odorata*,
I am sick with longing for my home.

Fragment

It is not a butterfly flying in the February air,
But a white feather lifted in an upward draught.

Since you left, and, since you left
The nights are longer, the days not light.

Preparing ourselves in shadows for the new life.

From the Russian of Osip Mandelstam

Heaviness, tenderness, sisters – your markings are the same.
Wasps and bees suck on the heavy rose.
Man dies, heated sands cool down, yesterday's sun goes
Out. On a black stretcher.

Oh the heavy honeycombs and tender snares,
Easier to raise a megalith than to say your name again!
I have one care left in the world, a golden
Care. To crush time's burden.

The mudded air like blind dark water, I drink it.
Time, has been ploughed up, and the rose was earth. In the slow-
Moving whirlpool the heavy tender roses, heaviness and tenderness
Of the rose, woven in double wreaths. She did that.

A Poem of Beginnings

In a world so vast as this such few survive –
Was it this that lay on top of us like a monstrous weight?

And the tapping at the window? Memory –
Look through me she is there.
And who in the realm of angels would hear me?

If I cry? Look backward once as Orpheus
And even the song is lost. We are well
Advanced in the new life, asking more.

Or, this reasoned light breeds pagan dreams, issue-
Less in an ideal world: Kill it, kill everything that moves.

No, but the reason of the waking dream –
Dante, if this is true it is a miracle;
If you made it up it is incredible.

Sand, pebbles on a beach: a few are beautiful, all
Rounded by the sea, moving to the moon.
And tapping at the window? A branch in the wind.

The Poem as Light

      1

In imagination a building, moving with the seasons,
Moving on its axis, and in the courtyard a tree,
Revolving with the motion of the planets
And answering each heartbeat in token of the time
When time, with sun and moon, stands still.

And by the courtyard crystal fountains, peonies and Mexicans
And music
            echoing the spheres of silence

Upon an instrument of ten strings, and upon the psaltery;
Upon the harp with a solemn sound.

Rain will fall and not fall: the dream
Of Byzantium interpreted and re-interpreted:
Eternity will swallow time and art
Become what is. Art is the building, moved in, breathed in,
All creatures move in this, and praise the motive, re-inhabiting.

    2

The dream of rivers, fig leaves silent on the tree,
    Countryside almost as white as green.
Spirit of river, of tree, tell me, tell me.

Scarcely middle air, in flight between cloud and birdsong
    Immortal spirits of river and tree,
Hurt as we, can rise no higher.

Dream of the spirit, golden birds singing in its branches,
    Golden throne lowered through the ceiling,
Do not blaspheme, my Father is deathless.

It was written over nineteen hundred years ago – it is the last hour,
    Spirit of the dream, imagination,
Air above the leaves on the topmost branches clear and blue.

Days at the Museum

    1

Rain on the windows gives the heart something to feed on;
Autumn casts a net of birds over us: it is better inside.

If you are happy, happy, if you are happy
The lightning sings. We heard an historical singing, on

Theorbo-lute and lute, on triple harp and clavichord, on
Mandolin and viols, the beauty of the world

Assorted, sorted out. Mosaic in gold and
Lapis lazuli: Annunciation.

   *

The crucifix is in the river: it sometime seems
The symbol is not so simple as a prolongation of the horizon.

Rich river. In fact. A gold ring and an icon and a crucifix
Cast off to save them. Rich river. Goodbye, my dear,

My love, between us there can be no misunderstanding.
The day's final image: an angel dancing between the stars.

   2

Octave spinet with silver mirror, her reflection pale
And distinguished as an animated grave,

Shadows dimly in the subdued lighting her survival:
The grave has no terrors save those to be seen

In our faces now – and, my love, my aristocrat,
In other faces? Survival hungry, nagged

By petty illnesses, never ill, never well.
Afternoon: sun reflected from wet pavements.

Go into the gallery again, listen,
It is an argument, always pausing

After the first sip, before the smile opens up.
He knew the ways into the kingdom of beauty.

   *

Silver mirror, mirror, mirror, were there not a form
Striving to be embodied, or our bodies turning for love.

Evening: Christians singing in the catacombs,
Or a massacre perhaps, solo and chorus.

Night: nought but a white celestial thought.

Of the Baroque

A raindrop rolls onto the next line, entire, clammy.
The monsters of the zodiac give off a smell of rotting vegetation.

The dahlias put out such a spiky assurance
It wouldn't be a bad fate, to be wrapt in their strangeness.

Cumberland listening to the women's lament –
But to be buried face downwards for daring?

The argument drifts on and another day, another skin,
Clings to what we know already.

*

A purple-black hand stretches and fills the sky:
The mythopoeic faculty at work.

A moon as big as earth infiltrates the horizon.
What kind of faculty is that?

When was the first time? When? For ever and ever.
The cruelty of the baroque: each angel's wing a cutting edge.

*

Intricacies of argument sustained in the solo
Add simplicity to simplicity to simplicity.

The palace rising, the vacuum, the
Cry, virtuosity of sun and stars.

Written in loss and read in fulfilment or
Written in fulfilment and read in loss the

Palace rises it has for instance
A green autumn fly for company.

An Anniversary

The trees in my garden split themselves in two
Saying: Look, here is the spirit of a growing tree.
Every day. Even during winter's so-called sleep.

The chimneys stand out clear against a blue sky.
Spring day in January. World, set
In our hearts. Again. And again.

*

"If the city had not fallen once, had not fallen twice."
    Five hundred years of stench, dogs drinking one another's blood.
I sleep like a dead man, modest man, no dreams.

A dark chasm between waking and sleeping
And time between the notes of a song.

A young man droning in the fugual perfect, waking
    Dreams. Gongs of monastic peace deafen us,
Dolphins tear the intervening seas apart.

*

One star is bright; not brighter than the rest; but bright.
I seem to see a flower held in blossoming,
Its scent a golden web worked in air.

Cloudless dawn sky. Mid-morning, white cloud follows white cloud;
A multitude of the heavenly host, keeping time;
The moon keeps my shadow on the ground.

He said, facing, if one may say so, the shadow of night and the stars,
"May this impatience lead neither to hatred nor to impotence."

    *

The fall of a tree is matched by the pushing up of white, green shoots,
    The environs strewn with human skulls and bones.
The attention of inspiration, in it

Art a living memory, and death is too easy
For this. The clouds, and the seas, have no movement. Today.

One man went searching for love and praised her.
    Gather the gold from her body; image of gentleness,
Harbour and treasury. See all the treasure that we have.

Poem on These Poems

Myrtle tree of heaven, white scented flowers
Of Venus. Look, I will tell you of a dream that I had
When speaking men were sleeping: moisture ran down the windows
Like rain. Outside, the full moon, one day old. It seemed
I saw another tree, laden with light, the clearest of crosses.

Love, love, the great love, or the unexpected,
My God my love I cannot see or sing,
There is no part left of me that does not hurt,
Even dreams hurt my eyes, sober mind's image.
Eighteen months ago the seasons

Became seasons and more than seasons, I had not seen
How slow death is, quick life – blossom
As flower, tree I thought we had done and we cannot die.

Days go by and the scent of the flower
Will kill me for ever and ever.

It is cold beyond the reaches of our air,
Our slow time; its trappings are gold and silver.
And poetry a voice, a voiceless eye
A dream from which I do not hope to wake. Love,
We find ourselves at the foot of the tree. We have always been there.

Ways of Approaching

in memoriam

in almost total deprivation we are all
learned survivors, the soft fruit calls, soft rain
a crystal, carried internally, a facet gleams as if
by chance, at the bark of a tree, glows in the atmosphere

when memory is of the future
then we may speak of fear and sharpening
and of love too more than of the fallen fruit
of the form that is calling and to that lovely form

Prelude

To live always as on the brink of leaving — but Goethe said
genius is patience — a crow is —

strong smell of wings or burning on the wind. The clouds
run for shelter behind the breakfast things.

                Great patience.
                Passa la nave mia colma d'oblio
                per aspro mare

                on bitter seas a string of images with
                song, care of crow, or sky
                of sky, care or crow

    "The whole concerto is
        one unceasing
            lighthearted warble,
                with no gloom."

    Il cardellino: the Goldfinch.

                *

                    blind as moles in sunlight, who
                    consoles us for blindness and sunlight

"Things one tells
     to oneself or God."

Yourself
          as image

                         And without
                    equivalent

What has to be
          burnt.

*

The wine matures, the colour and the scent, towards drinking.
The voices below the words — what might have been yells
with what could be.

But for the mind
to raise itself
a minute
          and the falling
back, unsustained
song, sustaining song,
and as at other
times, the changes
constant.

*

to the air
          a sheep's eye
dog dumb to the moon
                    and you, and you

*

No man, my name is
no one.

Comes into question, is called, friendship and the metalled trumpets
ring. They sound if they sound; I am not and no one is
over-fond of the smell of one's own
housekeeping.

On shore yes on shore from the bitter seas for the mind is free
for image if reading is not a political act

I have spoken and seen my words fall like separate bricks from a
                                                                                             dynamited tower
in lust or in love that pulls the heart to a new centre
I have and no one has
seen my children die

                              in spring, when the yellow
                              forsythia blooms

       and you are
no one and we both
          exist

more nearly

                so

using singing
to accomplish song
      the truth of song
to pick up the scattered
      pieces the clouds
run for shelter behind the breakfast things.

                    *

    wind blows

                    spaces

not on the wind, not
on the seas, on the energies

                    of love we move

a crow takes off

                    time which is death forming
                    space which is absence, no
                    man but also
                    is

is

                    the measure

bitter image

                    of patience, burning

and of this

                    *

at the limit of the known, enlightened / unenlightened

how many other paths unwalked and this
I've walked on twice before with a shiver of the new
each time to the limit, almost, of the known:

a punctuated silence, third time one tree
a mass of green from ground to sky gathers light,
a figure seen a long way off could be, un-

named, the centre of the world and in between
this known and this unknown, the exclusive, the vague,
in these gaps we gather guilt and love, and die:

imperceptibly the woods the sounds that come
from isolated farms scatter curlews
often unknown land, what I know of myself
what I know of this world and others.

Serious Exercise, in Honour of Boris Pasternak

Provisional governor of autumn the poem
Grows – let me, more simply, saturated, solved –
Of what it costs the heart to have a poet.

Frost and sun snap, a ledge of time, a web absorbed
In moral cognition, her face, loved face, blank, she did it,
Or I. Comforting smells of afternoon.

Or to live....

*

Some rooms have keys, others dustsheets.
We'll keep full bottles of wine as mementoes,
A gathering of light, impossible love.

Clear sunrise, attended only by children.
Bird-calls swoop down through the fog, parabolas.
Wring the sponge out, art, morning comes by.

*

Suffocating joy crammed in an eight-line stanza –
The lyric's now and self-pity hugs its cancer to itself.
What then? An epic lyric, end to end, the smell
Of death extended? Oh natural piety!

It's pelting it down outside, the moon melts the roadway,
I open the window stand on the lawn and choke
On roses and happiness as once
The silent sky erupts, a visible cry.

open house

the people inside in the rain
look out in the atmosphere of breath and bedroom:

framed in the window they see the blackness framed
hear breathing and draughts of air and the moon the moon
white or yellow or blood-red or the window

is a mirror and two people are
separate, see their night selves on the other side
eyes fixed and the frame defined, a picture

of lucid nightmare or the populous roofs
are silent, ash falls on the carpet and nothing
is the holding of a gesture

Report, Unfinished

the harsh rhythms of the frontier
have destroyed my ear   ,
a grating I try to imitate but cannot
has removed a great deal of certainty

     now take all this inside
what was it like before then   ,   in the gold
before this among these   ?
     keep that image warm   ,   that destroyer   !

out into bright evening sunlight   ,   these are the conditions   ,
                 phenomena   .

talk some

it was Faust   ,   not Ovid   ,   exiled
it was neither   .

excavators have been at work for the last five years   ,
nothing much gets built   .

a child's piano   ,   noise of the finger on the key
as loud as the note   .
phenomena
         I hear her footsteps across the stones   ,
         her footsteps that are sounds but could be made by no one else
         I hear her approaching because the sounds grow louder
         and I can time her arrival by the silence   .

in rarified atmosphere where under purple blossom
scent is mixed in vacuum but the bumble-bee is threading
and spiders link everything by the light
                 blank blank (blank blank   )
                 of the silvery moon . . . not old enough
to take nature as a woman

move into the rhythm   ,   don't sidestep   ,   move into it

but what is it that you can do
         apart from fear loneliness doubt

love and falling
         in love as often

waiting and a decision
         a decision is
                 waiting   or

60 m.p.h. in our constructed our
        time for a note from each bird then past
            sun bleaches hair   so what

so she came back and was the same and my desire for her
        and said
remember what you said about the other one a year ago
        there's too much remembering

alternatives ?   on a good day the rose
on a good day the language seems to fit
and not much to worry about
each man holed up with his own doubts

                                              round her shoulders
        familiar . so many confidences . I'd like
a strict verse form to celebrate them

        we must
                find synonyms for love
                              the wind
      lifts yellow dust up in the yard

                        *

first rain-storm for a month , the wind , suddenly cool ,
blows curtains half across the bar
until the window's closed .
where are you , and you ?

my voice
      divided
                perhaps it never was , but always will be
single
      finis amoris
                ut duo
unum fiant

                       some night
that low clouds move fast over the sky   .   in our village only one
kind of frog and granpa said this is a woodpigeon so it is   .
some detail come back almost lovingly   .   the ashtray
much in use   .   a moralist would have his work cut out   .
heavily disguised angels   .   heavily   .   no strangers to the job   .

through distances we've come to what end   .   like
driving   .   never like arriving   .   friends and talk
help   .   like the drawing that really says glory
(murmur   ) to Allah   .   like the
lighten our darkness take-off.
like construct something.

                       the world
stands accused and beautiful and images ambiguous
so the moon is deafening   .   it thunders through the window   .
the stars should have moved since last we did and maybe moved   .

as when the singer
                       in dark waters
                                          came
to the unfortunate islands
                       the soil being fertile
                       the message paradise
regainable
            and took it
                       to refer to here   .

"accept" it said and the tanglement'll have that sense
electric memory erased over the hillside or Bach
makes drunkenness sober   ,   she stood back
so a sparrow mightn't fly in the roadway   .   Meaning
and absence of meaning   .   something beyond
a wreck or an edifice   .   same difference on the wind
on the tangle   .   Intelligence does the job of no man

Poem

for Rilke in Switzerland

I have brought it to my heart to be a still point
Of praise for the powers which move towards me as I
To them, through the dimensions a tree opens up,

Or a window, or a mirror. Creatures fell
Silent, then returned my stare.
Or a window, or a mirror. The shock of re-

Turning to myself after a long journey,
With music, has made me cry, cry out – angels
And history through the heart's attention grow transparent.

Poem in Four Parts

the gardens of the fairly big houses are overgrown
white-walled rooms look out over them
and kind of blue flowers and the woods
metaphor rows of nuns and frightened novices
what to avoid and not to avoid when all want
and the woods a serious question give
no alternative to be responded to   ,   but to be
responded to people metaphor another
mouths after other mouths the smile etcetera
a kind of giving want now actively
loose enough to and the rooms stay and the gardens and the
gentle sound of exploding myths
moving bodies men and animals
and it does not end

and it touches I can feel the way I choke
loosened up but loosened up mio caro what depths
hysteria and the rest of it leaning my paper on what
metaphors there are   .   till the star that rose at evening

and I reach out for language and beyond and
hear or look and in the silence there comes something
too prone to lean even in glory
but when it is my beasts it is
end stopped and formative and definitive
or hopefully given the medium

someone waves from across the fields where pheasants
walk their chicks like a limb returning
now it is not so again ,   gold or gold-like ring
on her finger . suspicion . withdrawal . stop .
to make fresh start pattern of the moving parts
of nest as home comes up and a hare quivers
perplexed maybe it thinks it's invisible
but so but so it is revealed display of lower
limbs and breasts growing there aren't too many words
about nor should there be the ones we use a prelude
to more active silence figure or prefigure
arm moulding clay and birds light off across the field

within the animation of the universe
a burning line as is my duty / delight
of the year it passes it returns it does not
change what changes isn't desire
within the animation of the universe
no term set (same thing) except when this thing starts
"sometimes I am consumed with hatred" as the man
(Man) said a burning line which even in history
none can surpass slow healing slow to heal
or a new wound within the animation
lifts quicker than a surgeon's knife but seasonal
and laughter comes almost a parabola
I don't know what colour that is
sheltered under a tree in a wilderness with flowers
that must once have covered these Midlands a shout,
Sunday lunch, must come from the pub, hidden, how long
since we've seen each other; slight creakings
in the ceiling it does not matter
where you are but it matters   :   beyond

the importance of place, the sudden
change of sky; death from heart failure so
to say death by death; threatened so joy
to stay sheltered and suck in autumn's decay here
in the album and summer's prints in the earth
an oak tree an oak spray what
                                  in the Meaning of Flowers

poem for Jane

now again harvest time with cries the yellow
moon and then some is what's left
night riding high blue and silver
air full of waking not to suffer or take pleasure
less
suddenly the trees are still
and by what river is it possible to be lonely
lights and theme music of the big feature
by the smell of it , full moon in ten days
falling on the hedge when round the corner from the one
joy feeding on another and walk back by the jumping fish
same river how easily shame comes out of what
unrealised context ,   screen taut with epic and thin
mad voices we get there the way we can and who
would admit these shapes secure us handling
our lives our lives our true lives sing out of

in memoriam Charles Olson

or "love I never mention" or "love I wrestle with"
well whether they're "ors" or not or love
the mover or the move ,   the stain of it
in the midst of struggle ,   the story in the
mouth with figures ,   troparion and contakion the
man recovers   that lovely other alternative

a ritual o Israel Solomon and David happy
a world which prevents once felt goes before
the sun the many ladybirds this year
our lives our lives all welcome the happy un
happy hunter and unto ages of ages hunted
that lovely alternative
I lay my life before

Rough Tor, Cornwall, this landscape what song

this landscape what song does it bear to mind?   no song
the moor doesn't darken before the sky they
change, the both of them, from minute to minute
and as our ancestors in fear or anger
and religion raised weathered stones to note it
so we, content or not, are registers, polished
or loosened by the sweeping clouds and the songs we raise
are boundaries to what we own

"to live in this horizon as a gull and a fox"
goes the song and isn't needed this day
is held in hands already, perhaps the singing over of our loss
is song enough the moor calls, it moves and the sea
is never far, the shapes of men endured this rhythm
and were shaped by it, left stone or song,
rain linking elements
like a snake slowly changing its skin

and if after the pattern's as before what then?
we're not wrong, just insufficient, raised stones
now a part of the hillside, what rises may be dew
or smoke, there can be no vision
before they were, only after, when we've endured
I look to the end as the greatest cycle of love
a second turn, the greatest in the calculation
of our hearts

[untitled]

But that the buds are opening and it's Easter,
A fresh grave, flower-covered; a pheasant gravely
Watches, dressed in the same colours

The wind somewhat fresh and the beer good,
The moon leaves the hills for her own journey,
Leaves them dark, laying trails on the water

> Went wide in the world but it is here
> Went wide in the world and it is here
> Empires find form as readily as man, and lose
> As painfully, without the rights of a blade of grass
> What dance will you dance and fall to?

Bound by the curvature of space
But to graphs of space – to what else?

I see very little through the window   :
The reflection of this room in glass, and street lights

What I hear is perhaps
A dog and the wind. It could be more.

Perhaps also the blacker branches of trees cutting the sky.

lines from a notebook : a reading

these were silences and possibilities
of extrapolation   young flesh and possibilities
of extrapolation teeth snap
we take for real known terms

we go back from the red / blue lights to wherever
silence and obscurer promptings take us
(whilst dressing she closed the curtains, conscious of

her beauty) St. Gregory left the City,
the Queen of Cities, irritated by
interminable disputes over trans-
substantiation when what he wanted was service

America the weird and inhuman
which proves how inhuman....we try

I can imagine the dog's wise eyes
under the hair that hides them – of a life spent
and gold's continuance the condition the mere
condition of a poem and its furtherance –
I can imagine the dog's wise eyes

leave whatever city you have in mind
to name (if possible) where the light (possibly)
is clearer and disputes more orderable
and gestures are themselves and context

the water (running) and hills contending with
God's middle world are
                             the same the same but
the blank green grass receptive   .   and the sun
as before rises and falls   .   thus   .

Czargrad

I

to get to know the flight of birds, blossoming
of lilac-bush tipped with white flame
see the movement of the wind and try
to reassemble quietness from the creakings of the house at night, night
when the blood-red sun leaves the room I'd have written a lot
having lots of thoughts and memories of lots of people
in a book of hours, meanings, hierarchies
an Easter greeting always, uncertainties
of private death dispelled, carried closely, nourished
and protected till the time for it and the Poet
subsumed in the poet
      blue
flowers yellow flowers a garden a dog a stick
and courage
    but God decided differently
strangely unrecognisable almost beyond
where we've been the ferns, far plants, anachronisms
rampant, uncoil, sticky and rain hours on end
this garden, prehistoric landscape
          dirty public wandering to know
all cities to have heard and distinguished the cries
that women make and men in pleasure, in pain
the future stretched out as the past in faces
the god of grace floats high up over the cloud formation
hymns raised and lowered, seemingly not
getting any place, the common god
         what the sea
has to say, what we : after the blizzard they
jumped on sailors to get them in their coffins the schoolmaster
"consulted the elements" both flags we wave
in view, in view of, somewhat gaily : enough greenery
to get lost in temporarily
       reaching out, driven
from pillar to post of millennia blood
thickens, thins
     to get to know
the flight of angels "I have not loved

my contemporaries, I've loved their beauty"
"and pitied myself improperly" *cette pourriture*
I think I hear there the whine of receding light
more than in most
                      not much
jasmine scent from the islands
the stink of colossal crime
                        still on West Europe

    2

delicate the wind through silken corn
a life without compromise
hills over hills unseen the sighing of the wind
weighty in the palm
                      wisdom hovers, unheld
tangible, almost, between sense and idea
the cupped hands
                to get to know

and I could not help thinking of the wonders of the brain
that hears that music
the soft moths the soft hills the soft nights the soft breezes
of Asia .
and the music? gone, gone, but here and the form :
except, save (save) in the music of the line it is not, that's
the trick, mind
stumbles at that, not imitating
nature but man's art we heard
a priest chant vespers to an empty church (save
for us, spectators) God
in the City . the brain sticks . proposes
formulations :
                a city
                of squatters, drum
                of the dancing bear at morning, past noon
                both man and bear asleep in ruins, the bear's paw
                delicate . easy
                      a formulation

dome after dome and dome within dome
was . is . the caves within made
no space made all space having
rhythm and line and necessity
and duty perhaps in the poem one recites by heart
even to no auditors but beauty
a paradox in the very soft breezes
not apparent   for all
that one lives
                and is grateful
for all that without which
                and in spite of
in such plenitude the music
                comes of itself, were we
able .
      how make you hear is to say
how shall I hear . how shall I hear ? say it or how
hear exactly what was heard
                      in the ruins
till the time
        or this :

there is a flower
whose colour I cannot see
of pervasive scent
              the name
of the end of all things, in all things .
                        the poem . the City .

                        a flight .

    II

there are those who are prepared for the ruin
of empire and therefore empire endures
after ruin, a fish gliding to deeper water
there are those who are prepared for ruin
the wind a straight line from horizon to horizon

when the candle extinguished in its pool of water
releases the floodgate of moonlight silver
on shelf on bed on books on faces the measure
of our fall upward into night
iconostasis of our common misery
those who increased the measure of our love and left us
stillness : for memory is a contemplation
that rebirth is possible, that the song be established

where are they now, the people?
dispersed   .   the face of the earth   .   why not join with the exile's
recreation of what's gone, or lost, or never was?
                                                                    this
keeping house, a few precious objects,
clarities, the form of gratitude,
a gathered circle of light, strangeness
or the lifetime of a mind — hard fate

in retentive air legends persist :
songs made dearer when gone than ever they were,
sung by heroes, animal spirits
in what the storm disturbs and in what the storm
can not disturb, sense quickens
a painful building up of joy and love
gathers childhood's customs and the steady fields
sleek or gleaming, sounds border on ventriloquy,
an alien metallic power in this land,
gulls circle, silent, engrossed in the wind,
the composer returning to his people,
earth's face vanishing around him, *poeta
caecus*, this dream blindly dreamed
down to, back to, the face of it
the measure of it

a tiny world, self-reflected into infinity
the wind all the same about the house and words
hissed out in avoidance of error : what we're seeking
has little to do with belief
shadows violently on the window, thrown a hundred feet or more

and behind that between the turning pages a
shadowed space and (even) on the still white page
     a concentration of attention such
deep well of love
      bright cloud is
fixed
  that love
     is never fulfilled
but the ways
   of approaching
       endless

  III

  Morning breeze morning breeze murmurs
  on water trembles leaves
young trees above green branches
birds cascade
  sing sweetly the east
  is bright.
  See, already light's white
  the sea a mirror
  to clear sky
  light frost pearled
  the high hills golden.
  Beauty of moving dawn.
The wind's your messenger you the wind's
  the thirsting heart fulfilled

and that the stars them
selves on clear night the black
birds' nests and budding trees un-
fold
  morning breeze morning breeze murmurs
sparrows rise so much together
motionless with intense vibration of wing
     murmurs the breeze
on river flow

                    brown, green gradations
                                                silent
                white-flecked
                            sound, outward
curve
            of time, each leaf a kingdom, the wind's
your messenger, you the wind's
ideal audience ideal auditor the song
                        accomplishes the singer

            *

shouts from across the valley
raindrops pendant from the trees
the one manner of knowing : to reach out
as a leaf swivels in sunlight
angel's wings to the limits of sky
and still the roar in his mind
towered cloud domes, air cas-
cades, swirls as water
falls, from rock to rock the reverence
due to an icon :
                green of spring in the Carystian stones
                crocus blooming in light of gold
                blue cornflowers in white of snow

and I apologise to the blackbird
that there is higher in nature than him
to sound true note

            *

till the stream overflows its banks
overflows its banks and there is a face of waters
and there is a face of waters
and there is a face of waters

and so mirrored back to the known beyond which is
nothing   imagination   levelled

and beauty is residue after the bluebells
lilac   and the stream
                        name your realities
in silence in secrecy or as much
as the Word permits
relate them to earthswing, stars, a very distant
music through the plenitude of what is
to what must be in plenitude of grasses
shooting overnight two feet high obliterating
distance making the immediate vast
submarine rooms in summer foliage trailing
down rippled by currents a hunter
hovers over parkland, wind soft feathers
this day
          tendrils of passion flower vine round the morning star
counterpoints of rigour
clarity of the far white
walls picked out
                 vapour
trails, a routine with variations sun disc
silent   warm enough
for you? all windows
alive with reflections air
cool still though in breeze, in shade so
singing of first rain and
the rain drop by drop makes holes in my song
la pluie, goutte à goutte, the rain the rain drop by drop
the power to be humble and clear forsook me
this world of moods and voices around silence

      IV

weak in the light or a weakness in the light
          and so the caravan approaches
greedy now for Spring, the minutest details
the pageant flight of love's victims;
caught between sun and moon there is disquiet
the age   almost through mouths of dead poets

the angelic song burns with its own bitterness
that the hand turns inward to the light too often
and darkness grows useless, unused the trees
flame higher, proclaim what is, caught
in desire   stillness in the house, delight still
ascent and descent still possible, labour of precision
the crows' thick wings pass overhead; life in-
tensified, held now
as albatross wings are a part of the wind

    *

that the City exists
                      tints
of autumn brown and yellow, red
scarlets of autumns I shall never see but could not
in imagination better   and love
a willed deficiency of senses
how else could we bear, why else die   denied

no season is tranquil
recession of galaxies in a falling leaf
life blood   but shrinking the day
to insignificant concerns, deserted
leaves like rain

that the past the present and the future have no motion
no wearisome motion, steady thud of acorns
to the earth, information not opinion and
if we have learnt it is
that the hubbub is also texture of song,
the breath of exiles, survivors,
thought of home

    *

birds off across November fields   mist
startling confidence tricks   a heron   slim wrists
the people one meets   what's to be done

with love
spread wider   identity   you
are invited we never
knew each other hardly
for the years and circumstances begin life
naked   phenomena   dark, evenings, mornings
                    and
                         the
palaces the colonnades the prospects, domes, winter
dreams, rhythms of the world's desire
slanted sun circles to eye's limit
though the City is partly corruption, decay
a world of greys and greens and white under cloud
no nearer no further than fifty thousand years ago
by steps each of which is stable in itself
the City, jewelled in time
                         I hear the sky go by
constellations, star seams in a darkening world

          *

faithful mirror in a lake and then
wind ruffles the waters and we raise our eyes
and the image   language of transparent love
meditation   formed of exactitude
the City's walls   fail

slight stir of air through grasses
curtains sucked in, out, to the breathing of the wind
the body being anxious, seedlings attentive
Ararat   the smooth-tongued rain

mouths of hills shrouded
bare rock triumphs where water flowed
yellow death   heavy, nothing
keep to the shady the deep paths
rhododendron-flanked, gross rose from clay
out of sun

arc of hand poised before the other
                                          precious
red rose on the pillow, a sea of perfume
its roots intact
                 and that the sun sets
blood-red sated with its own weight
below the bleached fields
that all that is done
all day the drone of a harvester
next field

That is today

for Carol

[Untitled]

waves lap against rock
light shifts in shades of clarity
fastest movement ends in sadness   ,   creation's
epilogue lifts wings of reason   ,
useless wings   ,   imaginary
                                        imaginary wings
beat them
and they   ,   to whom we dedicate experience
had substance before it:
                      awash   ,   awash
Greek islands   ,   lucid bones of contention   ,   still
enduring   ,   I have the front door open (on which panel
of lead-lighting is the name *CLIFTON*) birdsong
and traffic noise   .   this cottage ridiculously
expensive   ,   town one way   ,   country the other
and this houselet too hot in summer   ,   too cold in winter
illuminated by our sleepwalking   ,   intermittently lit
by consciousness   ,   that vacuum waiting to be filled
in the time before time expands   ,   that fear of it   ,
emptiness before and emptiness after   ,   both full   ,   and
changes in rhythm needing pretty sharp attention kept
tendrils sways for a foothold   or shell
or hill-curve   emotion held in truth   thick green
dusk comes onto the tongue
fine dark steel well-tempered   ,   listen   ,
don't you remember days like that   ,   days
like that perhaps   ,   or look   ,   pointing:

the moors   ,   rain   ,   cloud caught in trees:
small catchment area really   .   when we
avoid talking about big things in case we put them glibly
and small things in case we make them too complex
so sheep wander along the roadside and water
flows down the gullies at last   ,   down to where we shall be soon

these years of death   .   that history brings death   ,   is death
frost-sharp stars and ripe fruit

wind tries for a clean sweep
and the kernel now opens with desire
sixth sense
           of the invisible

traffic noise as before
beech-mast pelts down

at the Stanley Spencer exhibition

the plants succulent   ,   distinct   ,   each in its own atmosphere
announcing planthood in a tended garden
with blossoming trees a variation on the theme
or fields again ripe with harvest
what language – or harvest – allows you to express
and then begin : start with fools   ,   a likely start   ,
wounded as chrysanthemums   ,   caught in our own shadows
though there are windows could open
and hands grow delicate in opening
the worst wound is love   clouds   ,   cloud over
as a journey returned from   or started

movement in three parts

clouds of witnesses nudge at understanding
now   ,   with light colouring of snow in clothing of images
rain falls on the Dart from a half-blue sky and
woods are sketched in by a child's crayon
and here we have
a starling attending Telemann   ,
harmonies brought to a triumphant conclusion –
subversive

        these pale colours almost blind us
and what can be fully described is

less than the describer so you came
to the living death of sea with gentleness
of hands ,   slept on history as on a bed of nails ,
dark ,   Judas days when nothing goes right
yet still grit for the pearl

                         meanwhile we
flounder happily in this sea of symbols –
further along the coast the land with its body
of red cliffs falls into the sea :
restoration of the beginning ,
not complete till the end free captive
in that unbearable time which is as it becomes

travel notes

impossible to be silent ,   impossible to speak
ritual of light holds memory of darkness
in itself and we ,   we cling to darkness .
that chestnut sapling about to burst into leaf
has more truth than I ;   burst of flame
to be followed by green ,   flame reaching
outwards and upwards ,   an offering of itself
road unrolled like a wet ribbon through the fields
and a heron ,   always the same one
fishes motionlessly in this rain
that spreads the light evenly   now are
all things made

river full and brown
concept ,   sound and invocation
coincide in word ,   in dusty blackthorn

some things so simple : these are the paths I walk on every day
there's where the dog chases squirrels
my wife breathes under the same roof
interpretations flicker about them : got you!

no , never , never simple enough for that but when the wind
                                        drops suddenly
now it's booming through the trees , now it's quite gone
there in that space is what I take to be a laughter
as the dome of Hagia Sophia ,
stone letting light through

the dog moves in his sleep , settling the day's accounts
above this square flat roof the sky
peels off layer after layer of time
vertigo no less and here am I
unable to settle
making a bad job of expressing joy

spring . diversion

this then is speech . in what sense ?
later I'll get on my knees , for the moment
all suffering and slavery and death
and then sterile cherry blossom
or mallards struggling to make it on our dirty lake

a long-haired girl leans against a tree reads poetry
so beautiful I'd have spoken if I dared
an explosion of greens : coming ready or not
again that mist of bluebells , where's the ground end , where ?

judgement comes unexpectedly , so does glory
ready or not ; the absolute is a room
without doors or windows ; sod that for a lark

young lovers kiss beneath an umbrella – the
rain as it were relentless , and here it is again
the decorative cherry
a hunger so fine that food's useless ,
the mind an intruder in its own operations
today I'd lay a bet there ain't no such thing as magic

I think the beech tree's going to play a trumpet ;
the oaks embark on an overture

summer seeming

everything can be grown from seed – only stipulation
is if the seed's diseased . this greasy turf , no
bowlers' footholds , how the childless also figure
in the generation game , dark warm words rise
from the mid-day soil cut across by a cool breeze , gratefully
gulp them down . summer seeming , endless
search for a rhythmic foothold , a familiar gratefully
accepted . provided . ask no questions . answer no questions .

now what a dawn unfurls , every surface
wet , glistening . the armchair just holds my body
though it could seat someone bigger .
the essential oil of the plants or herbs employed :
a couple of pieces a day . a day ! drip , drip ,
two by two , two by one , a cloud-growling ,
a green automatic and finally
no play at all today

for the rain , you see , a notation dotted
across every chair in the landscape
and perfectly neutral what the bloody hell
to do with emotions . birds dive about – dive
into a respectable dive , drink given
words gratefully , could be worse , a breathing space ,
smugness of fair seed-time pounds ,
it pounds and is not satisfied .

the sky temporary though it may be
fills in well , benches lurid , wasps wait
people retire to cars trees in vee
formation keep static perspective
as why not , flower-beds , crisp bags it goes on

image born in as insistently as sheet rain :
acceptance not enough   ,   inheritance   ,   continuation
why move   ,   why not move   ,   wind tears through upper branches
each atmosphere cloyed how can you tell
one skin from another   .   wind grows in violence

once
success is beauty

autumn sunshine   ,   clawed hand on the morning paper
traces explosions of desire   ,   the human
lineaments : she killed herself   ,   dreaming
of her Tunisian lover   the Canon
attacked for standing aside   ,   with God   ,
from the world

we were what you are —
you will be what we are

a bread strike a power strike — then sun strike rain
strike angels' strike? eternity   ,   that is   ,   today   ,
comes out to meet us with such aids

dog's skull dreams softly   ,   guarded by paws
dreams in no time at all

unstoppable splendour waves
work in one after another and earth
makes ready to sail

after sky

that is   ,   today

for home again

from night ,   not at all unconscious ,   once more emerged ,
three days of fog replaced by blue and blinding light ,
to offer as always poverty so heave
it all outside – that everything on earth
is substance and sustenance ,   gardens
immaculately silent look how the leaves
turn yellow ,   the white rose blooms on

not above picking up a few tips ,
boat wallowing through uncertainty as if
there's relief in northern vowels
their lives ,   the comforting fog not to know
where you're going ,   you don't need to

sudden shocks of light ,   direct ,   reflected
(age of double-talk ,   abstractions ,   hence
"soul-less caring" – wild applause)
what beast though can be in this light
not hostile to a heart-beat of all things
so you find it again and name it again
and it's new
that which moves quietly
                              hidden ,   un-
recognised unlabelled joy
                              wings needing no air
to hold them yet rather holding they
beat as waves ,   as heart
                            a rustle
                            a shadow of movement

Darwin motionless before a flower so little
affection in memory
late autumn breeze
                        beyond itself

Translations

Osip Mandelstam: Three Early Poems

1

Cautious, toneless, sound
of fruit from a tree
to the constant
melody of deep forest silence…

    1908

2

Your form was sinister, shifting,
I couldn't make you out in the fog.
Not thinking I said "O Lord!" –
It just came out.

The Name of God like a great bird
Took off from the wilderness.
Ahead, a dense fog swirls –
Behind, an empty cage.

    1912

3

First Football
  a fragment

Dreary matinée clear away,
Enter day, on bare feet.
Boys, playing football
In the yard of the military school.

    1913?

Mandelstam's Octets

I love the way the fabric unfolds
when after two three or
even four convulsions there
comes the sigh that sets it straight –
when that instant's near what
relief, what pain – and the sudden
shock of arching breath
sounds in my mutterings.

*

I love the way the fabric unfolds
when after two three or
even four convulsions there
comes the sigh that sets it straight –
and space, half asleep, plays at
sketching the arcs
of a sailboat regatta –
a child in need of its cot.

*

Rough draft destroyed, when in
studious mind you hold a
sentence not weighted by footnotes,
complete in inner dark,
and, under its own steam,
eyes screwed up, it holds –
it has much to do with paper
as a dome with desert skies.

*

Tell me, desert draughtsman,
geometer of shifting sand,
can these impetuous patterns be
stronger than the blowing of the wind?
– His ditherings and Yiddish panics
are no concern of mine –
he models experience on his mouthings
and gets drunk on baby-talk.

*

O butterfly, o Moslem girl
in slit winding-sheet, both –
a living thing and a dying thing –
what a weighty one, this!
Sharp-toothed, with great antennae
she went off, head in burnous.
O shroud unfurled as a flag –
fold your wings – I'm afraid!

*

And the jagged paw of the maple
basks in rounded nooks,
patterns composed on walls
from the markings of butterflies.
Living mosques, they exist,
and right now it comes to me:
maybe we're Hagia Sophia
with a countless wealth of eyes.

*

And Schubert in water and Mozart in the language of birds
and Goethe, whistling along a tortuous path,
and Hamlet, his fearful steps a kind of thought,
all took the pulse of the crowd and trusted the crowd.

Perhaps there was whispering before lips were born
and leaves swirled a treeless land,
and they, to whom we dedicate experience,
had substance before it.

*

We drink an obsession with causes
from glasses like needles, plagued,
hook on to a trivial hugeness
as small as an easy death.
And still, when these trifles match up,
a child keeps silence – the mighty
universe sleeps in the cot
of a little eternity.

*

And I emerge from space
into the abandoned garden of greatness
and tear this sham trust to pieces,
this knowledge of causes.
Your primer, infinity, I read
by myself, nobody else around –
your savage and leafless herbal –
your maths book of massive roots.

*

Beyond repeating nature by heart the eye,
hard as blue, has fathomed its law,
in earth's crust rocks are fools in Christ, a groan
is torn from the breast like ore.
Stone-deaf, what was born too early
reaches like a road arced into a horn
to get inside the plenitude of space,
the pledge of a petal, of a dome.

*

Sixth-sense, minute companion,
lizard's small third eye,
the monasteries of snails and bivalves,
murmur of shimmering cilia.
The ungraspable, how near!
Impossible to unravel it or catch a glimpse –
as though a note were pressed in one's hands
and one had to answer, just like that.

Mandelstam:
The Stalin Ode Sequence from the Second Voronezh Notebook

Alone, I look frost in the face:
It's from nowhere, I'm going nowhere,
Everything's ironed out, not a crease,
Breathing miracle of plain.

And sun screws its eyes up in stiff-collared poverty –
Squints at peace, squints comforted…
About the same as ten-figure forests…
Snow crackles in the eyes, like pure blameless bread.

*

Dead-weight of these plains,
Drawn-out hunger of their miracle?
You know, their openness, we
Put it there ourselves, almost asleep; the
Question grows and grows – where from? where to?
And isn't there, crawling on them, slow,
One we scream about in sleep,
The Judas of uncreated space?

*

O, this slow, this short-breathed space –
I've had enough of it!
The horizon gets its breath back, it's wide open –
You need a bandage on both eyes!

I'd sooner have put up with the layered sands
In Kama's jagged banks,
Have hung on to its bashful sleeve,
Its whirlpools, its edges, its depths.

We'd have been at one – for a hundred years, for a second –
Envious of the headstrong rapids
I'd have heard, under the bark of living trees
The thread-like movement of their rings.

*

World's lovely leaven –
Sounds, tears, tasks,
Yeasty accents
Seething
– And loss of sound –
From what ore or blood bring you back?

For the first time in life you
Feel raw dents in bankrupt memory,
Filled with copper, water,
And you're into them,
Not liking yourself, not knowing yourself –
Blindman and guide.

*

A little wet-furred devil climbed –
Well, where's he to climb to? where? – in

To the thimbled hoofprints,
Into the hurried tracks –
Milestoned air steals
Pennies from the village.

Road smashes in tiny mirrors –
Hurried tracks
Must stay a while longer
Without glittering shroud.
The wheel comes down at an angle –
It's settled again – not bad!

I'm bored – my main work
Jabber, twisted,
Interfered with,
Mocked, the axis wrong.

*

Don't compare: a living man can't be compared.
In some kind of tenderness, fright,
I'd accepted the parity of plains,
The sky a sickness round me.

I turned to my servant, air,
Expected service, or news,
Got ready and sailed on the arc
Of journeys that didn't start.

Where there's more sky for me – there I'll wander –
And a clear-eyed longing won't free me
From Voronezh's still young hills
For humanity's hills, growing bright in Tuscany.

*

How it burns, that feminine silver,
Resisting oxidation, debasement,
And quiet work silvers
Iron plough and poet's voice.

*

You're not dead yet, you're still not alone
While with your beggar-woman friend you
Delight in the grandeur of plains
And of haze, of hunger, of blizzard.

In sumptuous poverty, majestic misery
Live at peace, live comforted –
Those days and nights are blessed and
Sinless, sweet-voiced work.

Unhappy the man whom the wind bowls over,
Who, as if by his shadow, is scared by a bark;
He's poor who only half alive
Goes begging to his shadow.

*

Today I'm in a spider's web of light –
Black hair, whitest of hair –
My people need light and light-blue air,
Bread and the snows of Mount Elbruz.

But there's no one to talk it over with,
And I'll hardly find it by myself –
There are no such transparent, weeping stones
In the Crimea, in the Urals.

My people need verse mysteriously their own
To wake them eternally, a
Flaxen-curled chestnut wave, that they
Bathe in its sound.

*

Befell a fallen verse, father unknown,
As a stone falls from sky, rouses earth;
Inexorable – that's a godsend for a poet:
Can't be any other – that's it.

*

Mounds of heads, receding into the distance.
I'll shrink there, sink into oblivion yet
In the tenderness of books, in children's games
I'll rise from the dead, to say that it's sunny.

*

I hear it, I hear early ice
Rustle under bridges,
I remember how bright drunkenness
Floats overhead.

From musty stairs, from squares
With angular palaces,
Alighieri sang in more powerful song
The circle of his Florence
From tired lips.

Likewise my shade eyes,
Gnaws that grained granite,
Sees at night a row of formless blocks
That seem houses by day.

Or it twiddles its thumbs,
Yawns with us,

Or makes a commotion among folk,
Warms itself on their wine and sky

And feeds persistent swans
On bitter bread…

*

I love this frosty breath
And what fallow winter says: reality –
That's me, reality – this is it!

And a boy, red as a lantern,
Lord and master of his
Sledge, speeds by.

And I – at odds with the world, with will-power –
Connive at the sledge's contagion,
Its snow-fringed silver runners,

And the age'd fall lighter than a squirrel,
Lighter than a squirrel to the gentle river,
Half the sky on its knees, in cloud boots.

*

What to do this January?
Wide-open town, wildly prehensile…
Can it be I've got drunk on closed doors?
All these locks and bolts: I could howl.

And barking ginnels: stockings. And
Twisted streets: junkrooms. And
Idiots hurry to hide in corners and
Hurry out again.

And I slide into the depths in warty darkness
To the frozen tap and
Choking, gobble dead air.
Rooks scatter in fevered flight.

And I gasp after them, knocking
At some frozen, wooden box:
– Reader! doctor! someone with advice!
On this bristling staircase – let's talk!

*

The age's mighty sentinel looks on:
Stations, squares,
Commotion, bustle, just the hint
Of a raised eyebrow.

I've realized, he's realized, you've realized,
So drag me where you like:
To the station, that talkative maze,
Or to wait by the river.

A long way away now, that stop,
That boiler, tin
Mug on a chain and murk
Over one's eyes.

Perm accent, powerful, loud,
Passengers struggling,
And the reproach in those eyes from the wall
Caressed me, drilled into me.

Much of what's to come's kept close
By our pilots and reapers,
Social rivers and forest depths,
Social towns.

What's passed is not to be remembered –
Burning lips, musty words –
White blind's rattle,
Rustle of iron leaves.

*

But really it was quiet –
Just a steamer on the river,
Yes, and buckwheat flowered behind the cedar,
Fish swam in the murmuring river.

And I went to him – to his heart's core –
Went without a pass to the Kremlin,
Rending the canvas of distances,
Heavy, with guilty head.

*

Dream shields my drowsiness as of quiet Don
And tortoise formations are deployed, manoeuvres,
Quick, excited armour, inquisitive carpets
Of human speech. And words I can follow
Lead me to battle in defence of life in
Defence of country – a
Land where death sleeps as an owl by day,
The glass of Moscow burns between cut-glass ribs.
The words of the Kremlin are invincible;
In them, defence of defence, and armour,
Forehead, head and eyes in amicable setting.
And lands – foreign lands – hear the striking
Of the clock, sound falls from choirstalls:
– Slaves shouldn't be slaves, slaves shouldn't be slaves!
And the choir sings hand in hand with hours.

*

Like wood and copper, Favorsky's flight.
In hardboard air I'm a neighbour of time:
Layered flotillas of sawn oak, maple copper,
Bring us together.

Resin still rages in the rings, it oozes out:
Is that all the heart is – frightened meat?

At heart, I'm guilty – and at heart's core
Part of an hour, extended to infinity.

An hour replete with countless friends,
Hour of threatening squares with happy eyes:
I'll still have my fill, looking round this square, all
Round this square with its forests of flags.

    *

He still remembers my worn-out boots,
The worn-out grandeur of my soles,
And I remember his harsh voice,
His black hair, near Mount David.

Pistachio streets, tricky streets
Renovated with eggwhite or chalk,
Balcony, incline, clattering, horses, balcony,
Young oaks, planes, slow elms.

Yet the writing so curved so feminine it
Dazzles the eyes in its casing of light,
It's a good town, sunk back in its beams
In a young-for-its-age but aging summer.

    *

Chained-down, nailed-down, groaning, where's
Prometheus, helper and cliff's support?
Where's the black kite, yellow-eyed,
Hunting claws, sullen flight?

It can't be – tragedy can't be repeated.
But these lips about to speak,
But these lips lead straight to the heart
Of Aeschylus the docker, of Sophocles the forester.

He – echo and greeting, he was – milestone, no – ploughshare.
The stone-air theatre of times to come
Came of age, they all want a sight of the others:
The living, the doomed, those to whom death won't come.

*

Like Rembrandt, that martyr of chiaroscuro,
I've gone deep into ever more silent time,
But the cutting edge of my burning rib
Is guarded neither by those watchmen
Nor by that soldier, asleep in the storm.

Do you forgive me, magnificent brother,
Both master and father of black and green,
But the eye of falcon quill
And hot harem caskets at midnight
Excite the tribe disturbed by twilight's furs
To no good, to no good.

*

When my larynx is wet, soul dry, I sing,
When eyesight's moderately moist, consciousness not cunning.
Is it good for you, wine? Are wineskins?
The Colchidian heaving in blood?
But my chest is weighted, quiet, no language,
It's not I who sings now, my breath sings,
And hearing is scabbarded in mountains, my head is deaf.

A selfless song's its own praise,
A joy for friends, for enemies, pitch.

A selfless song, emerging from moss,
Single-voiced gift of a hunter's life
Sung on horseback, on high, breath
Honest and open, caring for nothing,

Honest and angry, but to get the young pair
To their wedding, blameless…

*

Rounded bays and gravel and deep blue sundered,
And the slow sail cloud-prolonged –
You're not here, I hardly knew your worth:
Sea grass bitter, a counterfeit of hair:
Longer than organ fugues, it reeks of the long lie.
Light-headed, an iron tenderness,
And rust gnaws at the sloping shore…
Different sand under my head.

Guttural Urals, burly Volga land,
Or this plain – these are what I have –
…Keep on breathing, where they are.

*

Armed with a vision of slender wasps
Sucking earth's axis, sucking earth's axis,
Everything I've had to face comes back,
I can say it by heart; and in vain.

I can't paint, I can't sing,
I can't draw a dark-voiced bow over strings:
I can only drive my sting into life and
Envy wasps their cunning and strength.

O if sometime even I
Could be driven, past sleep, past death,
Goaded by wind and summer's warmth to catch
Sound of earth's axis, catch sound of earth's axis.

Boris Pasternak: Insomnia

What time is it? It's dark. – It's probably round three.
Again, it seems I shalln't get a wink of sleep.
A shepherd in the village cracks his whip at dawn.
There's a draught coming in through the window,
The one looking out on the yard.
And I'm alone.
Not true, for you
In wave on wave of white break
Over me.

Prose Pieces

Most birds are myopic: the eagle-owl however has an eight foot wingspan.

— Proverb —

Living In

I

Every holiday I go to my cottage. It is simple, a two-roomed affair. When I have money I shall make improvements. But, whilst I am still reasonably young, or not yet middle-aged anyway, lack of almost everything often seems an advantage. The country in which it is situated is not distinguished. A few hills, but not many, a few streams, though none to give a name to. One would certainly not say that it is in a forest; and, although there are many trees, it is doubtful whether their density deserves even the title of wood. Wooded. The attraction is that from the immediate surroundings one can see no other house, indeed no other man-made thing. It is even difficult to make my cottage out, as you approach it through the trees.

Every holiday. The shorter ones, though, are not worth going into. Just long enough to keep things ticking over. The same expectations are there, as at the beginning of summer – the summer holiday, I should have said, the two are not, in fact, the same – but there is never enough time to settle down. If I told you about a two weeks' stay, you would not know what I was doing there at all. What I want to do is talk about the normal, that is the important, things.

Would it be too cryptic to say that the first week goes by in counting things? Things like tins of food, logs of wood, ounces of tobacco, gallons of paraffin. In the village, incidentally, about three miles away (thirty to sixty minutes dependent upon weather) where I buy most of the things I need, they seem to have accepted me. You see, I said "the village" when what I meant was the village shop and the other people I sometimes see. It, they, are there, and they know I am here; nothing to be brooded over. Incidentally. Yes, counting things. Money mostly, I suppose, to check on whether I shall be able to afford to come next time. Flann O'Brien deals very fully with the subject of counting.

Over the years I have carried a fair number of books here. Had to duplicate some of course. And the room is not damp now, no danger. And every summer I bring half a dozen or so with me, and paper. Sometimes a typewriter, sometimes not; that is a puzzling decision to make. The beginning of week two it always appears that no book is readable since I have left the essential one behind. It always turns out I am wrong, but I always think I am right. That, in week two, could be described as one of the attractions of the place.

Life? Unreal. I have always longed to battle out a winter here, to see, if you will, that I could do it, but the Christmas break is very short. Summer is beautiful but easy. If I had to plant the garden and gather all the wood I needed for the winter. Week three. The future. And devils gather thickly in the trees. It is then I regret most bitterly having come alone, feel most the need to be with people, feel the greatest desire to kill.

What one has least prepared and prepared for comes out easily, and the aphorisms which the argument leads up to are forgotten. Not much left of the argument either, thank goodness. "How do you like your world?" But confess, you have seen through it. I eat my heart, a little at a time. There is plenty of time.

Week four is quite different. By then the trees and the stream, even the sky, have entered my bloodstream. I am trying to avoid metaphor. In fact. There is even less need for food, if that does not sound a funny thing to say: less need to be greedy. It is then, most often, that I have periods of intense longing, and the vision of her is so real that the word 'longing' is purified, losing its absurd psychological overtones. The vision, so to call it, is linked closely with the landscape, so that, poor pagan, I half expect, as a reward, for bears to come up to me from beyond the field and eat out of my hand.

But confess, now you really must have seen it: these are split seconds, or at most short moments. Have you ever caught a painter at work? Say, a landscape artist – but then, say anything you wish; even, under certain conditions, a man whitewashing a ceiling. A painter. I never have. I am trying now to imagine what it must be like. I imagine there must be for a moment in his eyes an expression the intruder may often take to be of guilt. I imagine, also, this intruder of ours to be adept at jumping to the wrong conclusion.

*

Every holiday I do not go to my cottage. There is no money to make improvements with. Every morning, or perhaps it merely seems like every morning, I walk to work. Every morning I pass the same people; the villagers have become accustomed to me, and I to them; but who can speak truly on a matter like that?

One morning a chaffinch flew up from the grass just in front of me, and for several paces flew abreast of me, before finally making the wall on my right. But it was mid-winter, the bird was probably old or starving; there was more anxiety than joy in it. The road leads past the police station, and often, in the yard, an abandoned dog is chained and howling. The flames of the dog's whining burn to the ground the building I work in. In a split second. Week three is a long week. It lasts a long time. So long, indeed, that I must now have a score of poems I have wanted to put the same three lines at the end of, and it occurs that perhaps these three lines belong all by themselves, or if not quite, then that they would be most at home here:

> *we shall die*
> *with human dignity*
> *but with animal helplessness*

And where is the artistry here? I do not know. I do not know at all.

Or say there is a storm. Last summer there were a great many thunderstorms and one night it seemed as though there were four of them acting simultaneously. The roof began to let in water in three places, nothing one could do about it, and the noise of the rain inside drowned the noise of the rain outside.

Or say there is a visitor. Leaving a perfume, a scent, on the furniture of an empty room.

*

Imagine it is a nice day. Oh sometimes it is, sometimes this place is beautiful, the weather, and the animals, and the people. The paint is peeling from the walls, on one wall a white fungus is growing, on another, black. It is perhaps time to call this the age of the dream-wrestler. An alternative would perhaps be to call it the journal of the plague year. Let us have a conversation about it.

I want to put my head on your lap because I am tired. I want to go out and kill my enemies because they humiliate me and all I take to be holy and there is almost nothing I can do about it. End of conversation.

There are endless walks over the plain – undistinguished scrubland and distinguished trees. Walking at night is like driving in a car by day, the same feeling of travelling into, or through, a tunnel, a tunnel with a visible sky. It is not atavistic, or adolescent, but it is reminiscent. The air is quite pure here, but one feels that if it were perfectly pure, one would not only be reminded of something, one would remember it.

Rain and again rain. The days are warmer; flowers replace the breeders' coloured labels in the garden; spring leading on to summer, or to autumn via summer. And winter. The equinox comes and goes, as an idea. And rain. A pull, yet scarcely downwards:

> *A silence, as a filled sail.*
> *The crocus and the cypress conducive to sleep.*

II

Recently I went on a journey, like this one perhaps. It lasted two days, and the first person I saw at the station on the way back was myself, younger, waiting for the train to set out. Shrubs on a station platform have a habit of rustling, drily. And it seems to me that on a journey one has the right not to know what to want. I should not be leaving you, or if I should I am going in the wrong direction. I should be going to see someone altogether different. Also, I do not trust these men whom I have paid to move me, they are as tired as I am, with perhaps less reason to be concerned in what they are doing. Even the pubs in this town do not work, the people in them bring the whole of their private lives along with them, one has the impression that serious drinking goes on elsewhere.

The air is like iced water.

A rage, an almost pure, almost disinterested rage.

A leaf is beautiful, and its skeleton is intricate, and beautiful. Would it be simpler if we all went for each other with hatchets?

*

I saw the revolutionaries under an immense and fruitful sky,
Cloud-bank upon cloud-bank, under a most blue flag.

There was a tapping and a movement of all the waters of the world.
If it's always the first time is it also the last?
A nightmare carried through to morning.

Spring floods, the resurrection of the trees.
Consider the lilies, the sun in summer setting.
A glance at the razor stars.

A song of welcome and no song.
Words burnt into wood.

*

Storm clouds gathering. April crashing about. The desires one has left behind to travel at their own speed. If one stood still it would take months for them to catch up.

"There is scarcely one man in ten thousand capable of acting logically." A dictum, and, I think, for the man who expressed it, both a warning and a consolation. Cut people off at the roots and watch their restricted antics – so much by way of agreement with the warning. And that is as far as it goes. It seems we have pushed the splendour so far out of ourselves it would be both impolitic and spiritually wrong-headed to admit that nature is fallen.

The human face shines as it speaks of things
Near itself, thoughts full of dreams.
The human face shines like a dark sky
As it speaks of those things that oppress the living.

III

Listen : listen, listen, I want to listen to the rain, how it strikes against the window, lands on every leaf, and how sad it sounds falling on water.

The hedges now cut off, almost, the road from the country. The tunnel is green. It attracts. And behind the tunnel, we know, is great smallness, as if each man were wearing an iron band round his forehead. But that is merely a different kind of expectancy. As Trotsky said, to a feather people react differently, but to a red-hot iron the same. He had the time to say that. When a bird finds somewhere to perch, it is already a tree. I think there is no point in signing this. We have lost our names for each other. They are available for fictional purposes. And our love for all things?

But it is enough.

Most writing gets written by day, but the small part done in darkness is important. No, not by moonlight; in darkness. Children remember in darkness; the remembrance of childhood is darkness. Sometimes, always, when I'm tired, lonely, unhappy.

It would be foolish to suppose that everybody is not searching. And for the same thing, though longing can show itself as cruelty. Home is no safe image, except as a private thing. "Even in this stop-gap thing called art there used to be images that were safe, used there not?" asks the sentimentalist. Or the archivist proves conclusively that there were, and faculties are established. And here we are prosing on about the ramifications, and with the ramifications we could deal to the exclusion of all else. To hazard a final ramification – many have.

Going to get the tea this morning, round 7.30, there was a thick mist on the back field. For all the senses could tell it was winter, except that all the senses cry out it is spring, and an aristocratic day in the making. A bird I have never seen, who joined us about a week ago, makes a most distinguished calling at this time. I would like to know his or her name. Now sunlight floods the paper, and a perfume I know about is here.

You are deeply hidden, but you are beautiful.

Or

You address me so formally at times.

Sometimes, always. The glare is almost a summer glare, forcing the eyes horizontally along the earth.

IV

The lilac smoulders, more flowers from poor soil
In the evening light to the tulip festival
In the time when the vixen calls to her mate
And her mate burns.

The tulips crash open
With Holland and Islam, the daffadowndillies
Almost forgotten. How often has the rain on her hillsides
Moulded the helmet of hair to her head?

Rising at five
To count birdsong, at eight in the tunnel of spring.
At night in the dreams of exhaustion
I inspect the carcass, and the sky is open.

*

*It was that time of summer when wounds heal slowly,
Beautiful the world, and beautiful my desires.*

*The alleluia tree's turned green!
My mind is clear and dying.*

*A dog a cuckoo then an owl
Share the evening, wind at the window, beauty*

*That is gone, understanding not following
Longing. A puddle, enormous in the night sky.*

*

*Thunder an hour before dawn, half heard in sleep.
A way of life could last ten years; fill the air,
Fill it. The grass eats last year's wrecks,
Exact as the scent of the lilac bush in stillness.*

V

Today I opened an old text-book and read: "In the freedom of the world there was air and sun, and there was life, taking into account two percent of trace elements from the soil. Time ran neither backwards nor forwards. Drums, triassic or medieval, the herald's cry superimposed."

    Words, words, words, words, and again, even more of the wretched things. So that, in desperation, even more of them suggest themselves. So that.

    If men had wings there would need a ritual to guard against walking.

    The sun, the sun beats down. How long is it going to take? Perhaps soon I shall look up and she will be there. The wind drops, ramming the point home. And in the meantime, after that? Small tree.

VI

The projection was a projection of itself. I have been there, he said, looking at the moon, but of course he had not, all that remained there was a small pile of wreckage. And then possibly he woke up. Even the simplest action, the simplest word, reminded him. Which shirt shall I wear today he asked his wife, and trembled, it was as though he had asked where his shroud was. He then looked at his wife, and sweat, cold, broke on his face. Whose children are these? Yours, mine? Why do they seem so interested in what's going on? What is going on?

This, mister, is your garden. Those are trees and this is grass. Walk on it. Go on, walk, it won't harm you.

Of course it won't harm me. I know that. What a damn fool thing to say. Trees, grass, flowers. So what?

– The car won't start.

She said that. Do I own a car then? Now that might harm me, whether or not. Think about it. Don't you play games with me: think about it yourself.

Round, and back. Just one turn of the garden.

Bugger the garden.

VII

If it hadn't have been for the mild winter I wouldn't be here now to tell you this. Now that's telling you something isn't it? As soon as ever I put my foot out of bed in the morning, it starts. Now you see clear enough what I'm talking about.

It's like burrs we are, millions of hooks, or sticky to the whole surface of our skins, picking things up, drawing them in, attaching them. And more than that, insisting on doing it. Refusing to do anything less. Not that I lose sight of the actual modesty of it – starting from the "simple" things so a satisfactory pattern results. But the simple things that rise to aggravate here am I and all things. Moral is what I end saying. A nag. Truth is not the word for the feeling truth had at its moment of being. So? So brown blue white red and the whole spectrum etcetera. As it is. But how would that fit the pattern I've been mouthing on about these years? There, if you give me the description beforehand, I'd maybe agree to find myself.

To choke on paradox until the One Word (which will surely be a part of speech) is found: to be immortal because I am mortal, to be unconditioned and invite modifications. In the realm of "pure" paradox this soon turns to heresy: I am pure because I sin so much. God is my gunpowder because God is not God. The last four words were a personal statement.

It is not as if the pattern depended wholly on us, astonished as we are. In time; it is heavy with it. Who wants to die? Or more accurately, who does not want to die? Let's hope it's a nice summer is a good ending. It's not much of a beginning either but it is a context. Or it can be if it is. Let me tell you the whole truth about myself. And it will be more than that.

How To

I

1. To think that a man's art and his life are not the same thing.
2. To think that a man's art is a luxury to be grafted upon middle-class security.
3. To think that a man's art can be evaluated and that the quality of his life cannot.
4. To think that what one can do is limited by the sphere of the possible.
5. To think that anyone who does not risk himself can speak of anything at all.
6. To judge a giant from the situation of a pigmy.
7. To believe in the useful manifestations of the Holy Spirit, but to keep to scepticism as a way of life.
8. To spread corruption by assuming that what all human beings share is godlessness.
9. To assume that the creation is finished.

II

1. It always astonishes an artist to learn that he creates in order that other people may have likes and dislikes.
2. Those who assume that matters of the mind are but thinly disguised matters of the heart are incapable of doing anything about the former, and rarely do anything about the latter.
3. Parasites tend to think that parasites are important: they spend their lives congratulating each other on possessing such an independent spirit.

III

1. When a man wishes to destroy himself, he cultivates objectivity.
2. One cannot believe in society without believing in the individual: if one believes in the individual, it is not possible to speak of belief in society.
3. It is possible that the legal definition of death will have to be enlarged to include life.

The Pig and Whistle Section

And then what we start to do when we have realised all that. But does it make any difference? No, we all go on doing the same old things, it is just one complexity the more, though it certainly does intensify the longing to find, and cling to, one simple thing. One person, just one, in whom and with whom etc.….And I think that that is true. Do I mean, though, theoretically true? As the man said, the Devil stalks the face of the earth without resting. And who is this Devil? Is it me? Or could it be you as well? If it were just you — one could not get over that. Let's have a look around.

If you could record all the stories round you, and only do it simply enough. Like the man who said to me: "Ah but the sweetness of the first kiss." And it was his story.

To sell the house and take the wife and children round the world before it's too late. "How I envy you for not having these commitments." Or the man who bought five acres and a house near Wisbech for £3,000, and the man who told that wanted to buy a boat, and one of those he told it to had a boat. Or subsistence farming in Lancashire (Yorkshire soil too good, a waste of land on an amateur): a goat, and £200 cash needed for dealings with the State. And a room for friends.

How the neighbours seem to like me not so much out of humanity as out of a dislike for the other neighbours. The lady next door, "Oxford people", who wants to move to a bungalow with a big garden when her husband retires (new houses opposite us, completing the 360 degrees of eyes watching us, sold at £9,000), prefers me to the previous tenants — who didn't sound too nice I must say — and lends me her shears (blunt) to cut the grass. But there has been a certain cooling after the genteel lady one up also lent me her shears (sharp). Accents I suppose. They both agree about the people next door the other way. "Police used to be there at all hours, such rows and noise", or was that the people in my place before? – both I think. "The cat's in the gentleman's garden so often, I hope he doesn't mind." Though I do mind a little the suggestion that "we" shall have to do something about getting rid of my sycamore. With the cat, the cat that does such terrible things in all the gardens of all the people, I get on quite well I think. Occasionally she forgets I'm human and I have to dash off for a piece of Elastoplast.

I see a partial tree from a partial window
I cover your eyes and lips
to hinder or blind
we will not give time the presence to do that

Dear Paul, Swallows were not meant to live through winter. Love, Francie. And then through the stages – "good friends" "like a sister" "you must be strong". Until something altogether else occurred to Paul. Slowly, quickly.

Demands yes; expectations no. Surely you can see the difference. When he started three hour telephone calls at one o'clock in the morning, and kept threatening to kill himself, I didn't know what to do. You know, what was expected of me. I felt inadequate.

Ladies and gentlemen, I accept full responsibility for our examination results. When I reflect on those boys and girls who might now be at university or training college and are not, on all those who might have got good jobs and have had to settle for less, I think to myself: a good general does not blame his troops; the troops are fine. And we have a fine team here, only it has not quite gelled. That it has not gelled, ladies and gentlemen, is my fault and my responsibility. A good general blames himself.

Welcome to Friday Forum. Responsibility and freedom. I would like to see more of you wearing ties, and I cannot really approve of jeans. Nor can I agree to the practice of wearing sandals without socks, as many of you did last year. Perhaps Head of Upper School has more to add on the subject of dress. No. No. Perhaps the Sixth Form Tutor. No. No. Perhaps the Senior Mistress would like to say something about girls' dress. Er no. On your way out please collect one of the yellow sheets, a list of the hundred best novels, prescribed, or suggested, reading for the Sixth Form. I know that many of the things you could have argued should be included have had to be left out. Necessary compromise. Not on the Penguin list. Thank you.

At the first sound of the fire alarm, the whole school will evacuate immediately.

In living memory, in the memory that is of the lady historian of the county, the village children used to have to break the ice on the wells in winter, before breakfast, before school. This within fifty miles of London. And I have seen in documentary films of the area old men with moustaches like Prussian grenadiers carrying a double shoulder yoke, to fetch water.

If a man cannot think of a greater simplicity. Your hair, the way your body suddenly expresses you. *Déjà vu* and *pré vu*: I badly need a theory of time to put this in. Not a circle not an elipse not an escalation of universes, not not not, but a complexity so precise that it leads by poetic right to that I know about. A great deal to ask; without you I would not go about it.

If only you knew the Catholic Good Friday rigmarole: kiss the cross, retire, pray for the Jews, kiss the cross, pray for the heretics. Little soldier who has no mates hunched over his manuals.

The first night we got here I thought I'd have a little walk up the road to the next pub, take the dog for a run and have a look at the place. And I walked for bloody miles, not even a house let alone a pub, till I came to that garage at the crossroads and asked the man how far to the next pub. About a mile he said, so I decided to call it a day and catch a bus back. When is it? Half past two next Wednesday. Madge, don't unpack the suitcase, we're not stopping. Been here ever since. Made quite a bit of money here.

What most people don't realise about Hong Kong is that once English people get a job there they actually dread having to come back to England.

The house directly opposite seems dead, the curtains almost always closed and rarely a light; but occasionally an old woman opens a top window and shakes a duster, cleaning it.

Some remarks on the nature and origins of religion. With metaphysical speculations about how material could not have been created from nothing and arguing for the existence of God. Very open-minded people they are. Thought-provoking I found it. The church spires keeping each other in sight across the countryside.

made new we drink in colour we drink in smell
from a wild inaccurate world   ,   now evening
now night now

No, the monumental business was started by my father's uncle – you may have seen him years ago, he used to totter up the street every morning to his old shed over there where they're building the new houses now. And this picture was painted by my grandfather on the other side – every time I come downstairs in the morning I can *hear* the sound of the sea as well as see the waves. He was a captain in the Church Army as a young man, and wanted to become a minister and then he met my grandmother and that put paid to that. No, he was a joiner and carpenter. A very talented man, a bit disappointed because he had no real outlet for his talent – apart from painting and the like. Died without a penny that one.

Of course one could include many more unstable elements. My impression so far is that he may be completely irresponsible and is of very low intelligence. Yes, I'm afraid he's quite well-known round here. It may also be that he's become institutionalised. Yes, that sometimes happens to prisoners, ex-prisoners.

The difference between pubs up there and down here is that up North you're in, you're accepted until you let them down, and then straight out: down here you have to prove yourself first. Anyway it doesn't matter, Friday I'm off to London for a night out. When I told the wife she asked if she could come with me. "Not bloody likely." She's a good woman though; steps out of line every so often but they all do don't they. What are you looking at me like that for? I don't know which way to take you at all.

Yes Tuesday's the quietest night but you never know. I once had twenty eight landladies come in. Twenty eight. And they came in with absolute decorum and they went out with hats askew and lord knows…

Perhaps it will be that way again soon, when it becomes familiar through a habit of association we have learnt to know of as familiar. And so the games, the surprises and wilder thumpings of the heart we place in the chasms we have learnt to call the unexplored, lest the familiar bore us and we despair. It is a long way round again and to shine with certainty is a difficult art. Who has ever had any choice but to give himself over completely to negative capability?

This game is not intended to confuse you. You are not supposed to fall into the gaps and silences. I am trying to make it as simple as is fitting.

At least they are working, you will say, seeing workmen.

Partly it is cold and disparate. It could indeed be argued that there is every reason why it should be so. Let us avoid argument.

Down by the River Side

Always somewhere else, somewhere new, to go. A chance word, a chance meeting, a chance sight. Always this atheistical "chance"; which nevertheless alters nothing, salvation or damnation no nearer. I heard tell though that the heart is capable of purity at any time. And on that subject? I am looking at the cover of a book made in a foreign country, a very ugly cover; the country is, as it "happens", all but land-locked, and so are the colours on the cover, entirely land-locked. There now, as a substitute for purity we have always got those less favoured than ourselves.

Ships come in and out of the harbour, either under their own power, or towed in by the tug. When the rain falls it is often like smoke in the wind, in your actual real waves, or as if someone were pouring it over the roof by the bucket. And when it has gone I bet you cannot tell what it is like for everything not to be blue and still. So in that sense there always is somewhere to go.

And to go back to? If you wish. "And when I was old enough to smoke I used to light my fag over the mantle." – "Careful, you'll break that mantle." "And he touched the mantle and he like fell in the dust."

Make a model of the world, this world, now, complete in every particular. Take your bearings in it. The commonest ships are German, from Hamburg, but also from Denmark, Finland, Spain, Holland, Norway, the Soviet Union and one wearing the Liberian flag, a flag, it appears, of convenience. The largest so far however from Belfast, and in the evening we played darts with two sailors from her. They were feeding on a diet of Guinness and draught cider. The evening was noteworthy for a win on our part.

and on this walk incidents from other walks intrude
so what there is is the composite picture
of a walk, the idea of a walk within sound
and sight of the waves, darkness falling is many
other darknesses and many other people too,
a way of not avoiding it as certain
as the path there is or these birds now wheeling
concerned for nothing more than their life and nature
on the calmest of days as in gale sunset night

"I take the lyric as an epistemic form." So relax, do not defer nothing until what there is to do is over with and there will be a beautiful stretch of bare time to be let fall into. Or have I got it all wrong AGAIN?

Rightly considered. This "rightly considered" is a long job, and it seems getting back to it, that model-making is hazardous. Children are given models to make, and perhaps they set the pattern for ours. A model not of their own world, but of some alien planet they are given to understand may be theirs if they work hard at it. We work hardest at it of course. What do you want to build? There are kits available.

"Incidentally, very, too, in fact a change of subject…my wife's mother was editor for "****" (goes away to be sick and comes back) and maintains that she more or less wrote it. I refuse to believe her. Out of piety. Though I suppose she means grammar and all that. In which case I do. Believe her. I believe my mother-in-law. How about that?"

In Spring rain a seagull cruises with curved-down wing tips. And then the rain clears. The very familiarity of the scene.

Caleyo, Simon, Soviet Mariner, Pelikan, Navigare, Wakenitz, Aramil, Grada Westers, Outokumpu, Wega, Tourmaline, Ocean Blue, Nogat, Valle de Orozco, Madaleine, Jastarnia, Bleikvassli, Poolster, Hasewint, Noblesse, Sota, Emmalies Funk, Ivan Bolotnikov, Vaterland, and I suppose, Dynocontainer I, Dynocontainer II. And certainly the Gribbin Head.

The stream is a river big enough to float 3,000 tons.

A forest path through the forest: analogous to setting out to read a history of the Byzantine State, a clean white page, an impetus to restoration.

*Virgin and Child, Theotokos Hodegetria. triple harp with
the animal smell of centuries in tow. will
and lack of will. take then as joy from my open hands
a little sun, a little honey. seagulls and absence
of seagulls. a sail. the emperor in his six-horse chariot, gold
behind a knuckle of rock crystal. the treasure now split.
images of extremes and the song she sang – ravishing
such tenderness with songs the soldiers sing.
and the people who appear in poems?*

But the atrocities needed to keep things as they are.

*wanted: a plot to accommodate silence.
a voice in a babble of voices little used
to accommodate strangeness for strangeness
it surely is: I want what I do not know
that I want. a novelty? a recipe for
novelty? not that, more like a coming round
to it: treading a knife-edge horizon*

There is a poetry that goes through life as a strong wind. It puts spaces between words and cleans them and uses them entirely for its own purposes. It makes it less possible for us to get them wholly wrong again without remembering the rightness, or to mimic them without being blown away.

*I had an argument about the person
and the person's seeing: bad theology worse conducted*

The hand painting the sky in suddenly drops down and begins to deal with the temple's foundations in the same colour. Underpinning.

Rain and rainbows. One that came down and ended in the harbour, just out of sight over the rooftop. A seagull flew through it, fading. Two in one afternoon, one arching to the left, one to the right, over the hill.

And the people who appear in poems, or who appear at some such moment as the rainbow. Their favourite gestures, their mannerisms, some habit chosen to represent itself. A swan, suddenly, in the darkness of the estuary, named as A SWAN. It's easy.

The little black spot on the horizon grows and grows, it grows and then there it is, arrived. Ah! There you are! Klunk. Suddenly it's Spring and everything. Adolescent girls walking almost backwards from the pressure of it all. It's nice to be able to breathe fresh air, that's what I always say.

II

The woman walks slowly along the path. The bones of any plan before the future fleshes them. Pause to look or sit. If it's warm enough. The rocks fold and fold about. Somebody. A day for first leaves. Memory patterns of most unsubtle tyranny: an exact repetition of the meaningless.

What is it I read about the body temperature of birds?
Something, I think, like this — it's hotter,
much hotter, than ours; their more intense energy
almost an ideal, their every moment of non-defeat
a victory.
   Sluggishly, a greeting to the nature that,
being eternal to our sense, changeless, moves
more swiftly than ours, more surely. Our wreckage
is too obvious, the pause between performances too long.
Why else should we speak of that world there
and this one here as if there were a gulf to be bridged
by sense or ideas?
   There is no cure for similes,
or none I know of.

Each takes what he can, and leaves or distorts the rest. Probably a lot of fake pity is expended in bemoaning this. It is a way of avoiding responsibility. Go as far along the cliffs as you can without getting killed, and then come back.

a butterfly lights on the path
"I hope you see your way"
young grass is pushing through it

the shadow of a bird crosses
my hand, my face, two paths
pursued simultaneously

I tell you there is
no reality, only
a place of streams

land edge, red trees
bamboo groves by the road,
an amphitheatre facing seawards

Freedom as a state is creation, which is timeless. Freedom as a concept is the possibility of choice: – a framework posited, which time corrodes. Yet no revolution is entirely without art, the shadow cannot move without the body. But what is can be made to wait on what will never be. Not, not the men chained in Plato's cave watching shadows of the real on the back wall, but real men mistaking shadows for the real. Or men.

I didn't have time to get out of the chair. Just grab a handkerchief quick. Bugger it.

It was a parrot too. If you didn't know it next bloody day God 'elp 'ee. I been sent out to cut canes before now to get a walloping with.

You want a good stingy cane and hit 'em across the ballocks. That'll do it. You can hit 'em around the head as much as you like, go on all day, break your hand. Get the buggers round the ballocks.

Here's to the bull that roams in the wood,
He does the old cows a lot of good.
If it weren't for he with his bloody great rod
What would do for beef begod?

Enter a wanked-out lad of a painter's mate who'd dropped his bottle of linseed oil and asks for a bottle with a screw top. To whom our barman:

You're about as useless and hopeless as a bloody monkey. Bigger bloody liar than Ananias. You think you're sleeping like a pig in a feather bed. Bloody shower. You're so low – if you were on ten foot stilts and wearing a top hat you'd be able to crawl under a snake's tit.

And when he'd gone:

I'm no stranger to the truth, I just don't like it very much.

The barman (alias drinker's labourer) served from 1914 to 1921 in the Royal Navy, had his ship blown from under him seven times, during which period he had 48 hours' leave, then served till 1948 in the Merchant Navy, and is now back. They don't know they're born.

A sun-haze obscures the farther hills,
triumphant tiredness of the fully emerged
leaves: the laws of nature take their course.

In that field there an enclosure, the metal fence
overgrown, and in it a stone commemorating
heaven knows what, something we've passed by long before
and forgotten, but the stone said we knew.

The day the Sophia Perovskaya sailed out, a blue, calm day, she used her siren repeatedly (Soviet sailors talk to each other excitedly, indignantly, through megaphones), the bow waves made a pattern, the pattern drew wider and rocked the swans, then the dinghies, slap slap, and then the quay (built for a royal visit that never materialised, it collapsed 24 hours before said non-event, and is now under extensive reconstruction) lap lap. From a receding white silhouette flying an apparently red flag from her stern.

III

"the people of God with you and all England over, who have wrestled with God for a blessing."

our nature changes which side to the world, which world
shall I choose, bewildered,
as we tell adolescents for their illumination
that they are, shaken, perhaps the wrong size engine
for the frame, the past can't always lead us on
to the same questioning

Clouds forming, being pushed up meeting land, land in raining cloud.
"….so that the mercies which the Lord hath given may not be cast away."

this light this light I speak about in virtue whereof….
plunged into darkness, a stream winding tortuously
but silver through the green, the pleasant hills
there are images of light and there is darkness
then there is light

"I pray God to teach this Nation what the mind of God may be in all this, and what our duty is."

Cloud shadow dark on the sea, the wind as white.

Notes

The dates of composition are taken from the *Notebooks* donated to University of Cambridge Archives by Carol Riley Brown.

Ancient and Modern (Grosseteste Press 1967)

'Pentecost': 30-31 May 1966;
'After the Music': 10 June 1966;
'This Time of Year': October 1966.

What Reason Was (Grosseteste Press 1970)

'For Gordon and Hélène Jackson': the painting of St. Onouphrios is by Gordon Jackson, and appears on the cover of this volume;
'The Full Moon is Bathing these Fields': 21-24 July 1967;
'A Picture: an Historical Perspective': 24 June 1967;
'Song': August 1967;
'Dream Poem': 12 October 1967;
'A Birthday Poem for One Person, and Hence for Others': 30 October 1967;
'The Shortest Day, Riding Northward': December 1967;
'The Attraction': January 1968;
The World Itself, the Long Poem Foundered': January 1968; first published in *2R2* (*Resuscitator,* second series), August 1968. In the first publication the poem existed as four sections. The first two had three two-line stanzas and the second two had two two-line stanzas. The final nine lines were added for book publication.
'Fragment': February 1968;
'A Poem of Beginnings': August 1968; first published in *The Park* ed. Andrew Crozier, Summer 1969.
'The Poem as Light': June 1968;
'Days at the Museum': originally titled 'A Day' and dated 15 September 1968;
'Poem on these Poems': December 1968.

Ways of Approaching (Grosseteste Press 1973)

'Serious Exercise, in Honour of Boris Pasternak': October 1969;
'Report, Unfinished': first published as a 36 line longer poem in Kris Hemensley's *Earthship 1* October 1970;
'Poem for Rilke in Switzerland': December 1969;
'Rough Tor, Cornwall, this landscape what song': 20 January 1972;
'Untitled': 18 April 1972.

Czargrad

In Archive S.O. Book 121: "This poem started in England, then it and I progressed to Constantinople (not, as a friend of a friend did not write, Istanbul). Thus the title is the Russian name for Constantinople, a name I have heard used in the City. There is a quotation from Rilke's *Malte Laurids Brigge*, and, as it so happens, along the way, from William Carlos Williams' *The Desert Music*. And now I don't know what use this note can be. But there you go. Tell me, gentle reader, have you ever crapped in a church and watched tourists take snapshots of the ordure?"

That is Today (Pig Press 1978)

'spring . diversion': 12-13 May 1977;
'summer seeming': September –October 1977;
'for home again': 26 October 1977.

Translations

'Osip Mandelstam: Three Early Poems' first published in *Grosseteste Review Vol. I, No. 2*, autumn 1968.

Prose

'How To' was first published in *Grosseteste Review Vol I, No. 2*, autumn 1968.

A list of John Riley's works

Ancient and Modern, Grosseteste Press 1967
What Reason Was, Grosseteste Press 1970
Correspondences, The Human Constitution 1970
Ways of Approaching, Grosseteste Press 1973
Prose Pieces, Grosseteste Press 1974
Mandelshtam's Octets, Grosseteste Press 1976
That is Today, Pig Press 1978
a meeting, Stingy Artist 1978
Stalin Ode Sequence, Rigmarole of the Hours 1979
The Collected Works (ed. Tim Longville), Grosseteste Press 1980
Selected Poems (ed. Michael Grant), Carcanet Press, 1995

www.ingramcontent.com/pod-product-compliance
Lightning Source LLC
Chambersburg PA
CBHW031154160426
43193CB00008B/367